AF263001

There Your Heart Will Be

Essays In Faith and Literature

Gordon Leah

There Your Heart Will Be

Essays In Faith and Literature

Newbold Academic Press

Author:

Gordon Leah

Editor:

John Baildam

Graphic design:

Any Kobel, Switzerland

Layout:

Manfred Lemke

Printing:

INGRAM

ISBN 978-0-9932188-8-0, Softcover

Contents

Preface

I first met Dr Gordon Leah in the summer of 1989 in the offices of the University of London Schools Examinations Board (now Edexcel). I had just been appointed to replace Gordon, who was stepping down after serving for a number of years as Chief Examiner, Advanced Level German. It soon became apparent that we were both able to share our Christian faith and experience with each other – unusual in a world where the expression of faith is often noted as a weakness. Gordon and I have kept in regular contact with each other in a variety of capacities over the almost three intervening decades. I have always been grateful for his wisdom, his loyal support, his friendship, and the many shared meals and solid discussions we have enjoyed.

Born in Cheadle Hulme, Cheshire, as the son of a bank official, Gordon attended William Hulme's Grammar School in Manchester before earning a State Scholarship and Open Exhibition in Modern Languages to Jesus College Cambridge. On completion of his first degree and his Certificate of Education, Gordon taught at Mill Hill School, London, becoming Head of Languages at Chipping Norton Comprehensive School, Oxfordshire, and subsequently Head of

Modern Languages at King's School, Worcester. Gordon is married to Gill, and they have two children and five grandchildren.

As a result of research undertaken while teaching, Gordon was awarded a PhD in 1978. His thesis was 'The Theme of Purity in Heinrich von Kleist', a late eighteenth-century German literary figure whose grave on the banks of the Wannsee I visit whenever I am in Berlin.

Gordon has written a number of texts and articles in the area of German language and teaching. Some ten years ago he wrote two impressive meditations based on the stained glass windows in Malvern Priory and Hereford Cathedral.

Tragedy in Gordon's family life led to a loss of his Christian beliefs for some time in the 1990s. We are grateful that Gordon found his way back to faith some years later and he continues to serve God as a committed Christian and lay preacher in the Methodist tradition, co-ordinating house group meetings and writing courses for discussion.

Since 2002 Gordon has had a number of articles published by national Christian journals in the area of literature and the Christian faith. When I met Gordon for a meal some months ago in a quiet rural Worcestershire hostelry, I suggested to him that he release some of his articles for us to publish in one volume through Newbold Academic Press. My own interest in German literature in particular, and my own desire to link secular writings with my own Christian faith, fanned my excitement for this project. Gordon went along with the proposal immediately and subsequently obtained permission from his various individual publishers for his articles to feature in this new volume.

Gordon lists his hobbies as Church, reading, travel, family, and watching as well as being an armchair commentator on sports.

I pray that the readers of this volume will be blessed by Gordon's insights into literature and the Christian faith.

Dr John Baildam
Principal
Newbold College of Higher Education
Binfield
Berkshire

December 2016

Introduction

When my beliefs deserted me in the spring of 1996, my first feeling was of relief. 'At least you don't have to pretend any more. You don't have to try to pray any more', I told myself. I had tried in vain to maintain my roles within the church community, as preacher, house group leader and church steward (many years previously), but my experience of severe illness in the family and the traumatic death of my brother had meant that I parted company from my official beliefs. The resulting fault-line opened up and swallowed all my beliefs except, strangely enough, an enhanced belief in God's created world. I felt that God had indeed created the world, but had then abandoned us to our fate and left humanity to fend for ourselves.

My initial relief changed into sorrow at what I had lost of my traditions and a sense of acute bewilderment that what I had previously believed and practised might simply be a consequence of a romantic imagination and a desire for groundless spiritual consolation. I decided that I did not enjoy my new position and wanted to return to faith, but when for instance I heard a reading from the Sermon on the Mount and found that I could literally not grasp any sense of its content, I remembered that I had led a series of sessions on that very subject just a few months previously in my house group! I know that I had to wait, while attempting to encourage my return to faith with various little helps such as short texts, cards, bookmarks, conversations with friends, and the occasional, well-planned church attendance. After a period of about six years, my faith gradually returned, but my roles had changed. I returned to church attendance and rejoined a house group, but could no longer preach. I had learned to respect more and more the views of doubters and unbelievers.

It was then that I started to put my thoughts on paper in a series of articles, under the encouragement of a church friend, finding that I could take literature as a basis of my reflections and hope to draw inspiration from the works I read, many of which were not overtly Christian. This started in 2003, and has led to a stream of articles published in six national Christian journals. As a former teacher of languages, I had published four school texts in German and several articles for educational journals on issues concerning language education. When I was invited during 2015 to turn my articles into a book, I insisted that they should be my published pieces that had been accepted by editors and peer reviewers, rather than the other pieces scattered around my hard drives which I like, but which were inevitably trial runs, sometimes failed attempts. I have also decided, probably because of my strong preference for the printed word, that all the pieces should be articles that have appeared in print, not only online. There are altogether fifteen pieces that appeared between 2004 and 2015, and I have stated beneath each piece the date and journal of publication. All biblical references in the articles in the collection are to the New International Version.

The first three pieces, which form Part One 'From the Wilderness', were written very much in the wake of and often during my 'wilderness' period after 1996 and particularly reflect the dilemmas and issues I was facing during those years. I wish to thank all the editors for their encouragement and approval of my publications, and also to thank various friends for their encouragement, primarily Malcolm Braddy for his initial encouragement to me to publish articles rather than try to write a book at once; Dr John Baildam, Principal of Newbold College of Higher Education, for his encouragement to publish these fifteen pieces as a book now; and the editorial staff at Newbold for their work on the production of this book. And of course I wish to thank my wife, Gill, for her patience as a good listener and her forbearance while I have spent hours on the computer.

One word on the choice of title for this collection. The title is taken from one of the chapters, 'There Your Heart Will Be'. In some words from near the end of Jesus' recorded sayings in the Sermon on the Mount, we read 'Where your treasure is, there your heart will be also'. My conviction is that true religion is found in the response of the heart of a person, in a person's genuine, heartfelt wish to do what she sees as God's wish for her, which is beyond all doctrine, dogma and laws, and where religion and service are well-nigh instinctive and second nature. And if such religion and faith are, as with most of us, beyond our capacity to sustain, my sincere hope is that those who read these pieces, which are of varying lengths and depths, will find some value for their lives and will appreciate that their often unorthodox approach may, after all, be a means of approaching the God who may frequently be elusive and hidden, but who ultimately in His grace does not reject those who turn to Him.

Biographical statement

Dr Gordon Leah publishes on matters of Christian faith with reference to literature. He is a retired teacher of languages and lay preacher. He lives in Worcester, UK.

Part One: From the Wilderness

The Gift of Forgetfulness
Thoughts on Chapter 7, 'The Piper at the Gates of Dawn', in Kenneth Grahame's *The Wind in the Willows*[1]

It was a very cold day in Cambridge in November 1955. I was out in the early morning, dressed in pyjamas, but with my tracksuit on underneath to keep out the cold. I was going round from house to house in the back streets of the city, collecting for Poppy Day. It was my first term at the University. As I went round a calming reassuring feeling came over me. I was experiencing a form of Wesleyan awakening. In fact, I felt my heart 'strangely warmed', as John Wesley put it back in 1738. After years of religious influences in my Church at home, I was experiencing what seemed to me to be my first moment of truly personal Christian conviction that God loved me.

When my convictions left me over forty years later, I was left confused and bewildered. After the initial shock, I felt cheated. Was my entire experience of the previous decades simply a lie or an illusion? Had I experienced a religious awakening at all? I had not wanted to lose my convictions. Was God toying with me and my experience? Had I been fondly nourishing religious dreams over so many years, spending hours as a local preacher in the preparation of fantasy thoughts and imaginings, trying to pray into a void from which no answers could possibly come because the call had been merely a dream? I still believed in God as Creator, so I could still blame Him for what I thought had happened, but nothing else remained.

'Where is the blessedness I knew/When first I saw the Lord?', said the hymn writer, William Cowper, so long ago. A curtain had fallen shutting out Jesus and any manifestations of His presence or work in the world. An experience of the Holy Spirit, whether gentle or intense, no longer had any meaning. My entire religious and mental world had existed in my mind alone.

Kenneth Grahame's *The Wind in the Willows* is at first sight an unlikely source of help, a work I had never read as a child, but which I thought might therefore open up new areas of thought to me. I read it again as I was finding my beliefs gradually returning to me. I found that one part of the book revealed to me much about the nature and purpose of intense spiritual experience, such as I had experienced in my early weeks as a student.

When I had finished reading the book, I at once re-read the central chapter 7 entitled 'The Piper at the Gates of Dawn' that had spoken to me so clearly. It is the shortest chapter in the book, isolated in the middle between the chapter which deals with Toad's sentencing to prison and the one which covers his escape and further adventures. The mysterious chapter 7 appears to have no relation to any of the other chapters or incidents in the story, but is the moment in the book where the wind in the willows of the title comes to have a significance not featuring elsewhere. It introduces us to an element of spiritual mystery surrounding the characters of the Otter and the Baby Otter who goes missing, causing the Rat and the Mole to join the hunt in search of him.

The Baby Otter, Little Portly, is in the habit of disappearing for short periods, but this time he has been missing for several days and his father in his anxiety is keeping vigil on the river to save his child from the rising waters coming down through the weir. He has taken up his post at the point where he used to teach his little one to fish, and he is hoping that Little Portly will eventually make for that spot that he loves. The Rat and the Mole set off down the river in the hope of finding the baby. As they paddle along the river, the atmosphere changes. It is night and dawn approaches. The description becomes more eerie than at any other time in the story, and the changing time of night is described in lyrical terms that presage some supernatural intervention and miracle. As the horizon becomes clearer, they hear the piping of a bird and immediately Rat senses a sound that he has not heard for a very long time and that arouses in him a renewed longing. The piping of the bird seems to have unleashed a distant bubbling piping sound of sweet music, which almost at once starts to fade. Mole can hear nothing but the sound of the wind in the reeds, rushes and osiers.

As the dawn light illuminates the scene more and more clearly, Rat becomes increasingly aware of the 'heavenly music'. The scene becomes significantly infused with a mood of expectation of supernatural intervention as they approach a small island. 'Reserved, shy, but full of significance, it hid whatever it might hold behind a veil, keeping it till the hour should come, and with the hour, those who were called and chosen' (114). The island seems to be a place apart, cut off from the main stream, a holy of holies where 'He' can be encountered, a haven for the initiated and the chosen. 'This is the place of my song-dream, the place the music played to me,' whispered the Rat, as if in a trance. 'Here, in this holy place, here if anywhere, surely we shall find Him!' (115).

Mole too is aware of the nearness of 'some august Presence' and when he turns to look for Rat, he sees him looking cowed and terrified. Mole then sees something that eludes his friend at that instant.

> He looked in the very eyes of the Friend and Helper;
> saw the backward sweep of the curved horns […] the
> stern, hooked nose between the kindly eyes that were
> looking down on them humorously […] the long
> supple hand still holding the pan-pipes […] saw, last of
> all, nestling between his very hooves, sleeping soundly

in entire peace and contentment, the little, round,
podgy, childish form of the baby otter (116).

On this island, the holy of holies, the baby is being protected in perfect peace by the figure of the demigod Pan, who has just ceased blowing his pipes. But it is not a Pan who inspires sudden bursts of terror and panic; it is a genial, whimsical, smiling Pan, certainly the god of flocks and the shepherds, but who, despite his horns that clearly identify him as the legendary god inhabiting and protecting his natural world, in his kindliness, more than a little resembles the Good Shepherd of the Christian Gospel.

Rat, who has not yet seen the horned Protector, is afraid, but reluctant to admit it, but Rat and Mole bow down and worship, just as Rat suddenly sees the slumbering otter, lying alone and peaceful. Mole and Rat experience different visions at different times, and the only thing Rat sees of the 'Friend and Helper' are his large hoof-marks. By that time, the baby otter has woken up, bewildered and fearful, until comforted by his father's friends.

They take him back to his father who welcomes him back joyously, running along the bank to meet his child. As Rat and Mole contemplate the end of their quest, their reactions seem to have reversed. Mole, through his tiredness, hears the distant music that Rat has heard previously, and Rat can only vaguely distinguish the words in the sounds which recede into the soft whispering of the reeds, which Mole had heard originally.

Rat now recalls the words that he had heard long ago and is now striving to decipher. The words are gradually becoming clearer to him: *'Lest the awe should dwell - And turn your frolic to fret - You shall look on my power at the helping hour - But then you shall forget!'*

Rat now hears the reeds taking up the refrain and murmur the words 'Forget, forget'. The sound then dies away in a whisper before the voice returns: *'Lest limbs be reddened and rent - I spring the trap that is set - As I loose the snare you may glimpse me there - For surely you shall forget!'*

He urges Mole to row nearer the reeds, but the voice grows fainter every minute: *'Helper and healer, I cheer - Small waifs in the woodland wet - Strays I find in it, wounds I bind in it - Bidding them all forget!'* (120)[2]

When Mole asks what the words mean, Rat has to admit his ignorance: he has simply passed the words on as they came to him. But when the words now become clearer to him, they then fade immediately and he is unable to say more. When Mole looks at him again, Rat has fallen asleep weary from his efforts at recollection, but blissful at the memory of them.

The words have slipped in and out of Rat's conscious thoughts, and can only be recalled briefly in snatches. And he has to fall asleep, to sleep on the awareness he has experienced. The clue to the experience has already been signalled just before Rat espies the sleeping baby otter. A light breeze caresses their faces. The text continues:

> And with its soft touch came instant oblivion. For this is the last best gift that the kindly demigod is careful to bestow on those to whom he has revealed himself in their helping: the gift of forgetfulness. Lest the awful remembrance should remain and grow, and overshadow mirth and pleasure, and the great haunting memory should spoil all the after-lives of little animals helped out of difficulties, in order that they should be happy and light-hearted as before.

Their experience has left them drained and exhausted. It has been such an elevated onrush of spiritual power that they have only been capable of withstanding a moment, a brief, but definite, though only vaguely defined awareness. This moment in the story is never recalled later. The scene acts in isolation. The baby otter's experience and the focus on the lives of the otter and his family are immediately forgotten. The feeling of awe and terror, the saving of the strays, the binding of the wounds, the helping and healing, all are too much for mortals to bear for longer than a minute and a glimpse, because mortals are destined to enjoy mirth and happiness, not to dwell on what is unsustainable. This thought finds an echo in the scene The Magic Ring from Kenneth Grahame's collection of stories *Dream Days*, like *The Wind in the Willows* also written in 1908, in which he writes, though in a much lighter vein: 'If the gods are ever grateful to man for anything, it is when he is so good as to display a short memory.'[3]

During my years of exile from belief I realised that, in my search for understanding and explanations over a long time, I had tried to demystify what must remain hidden and revealed to us only in snatches, handed down as it has been received, in trust, slipping in and out of our conscious awareness, sometimes clearly heard and visible, often masked from us, but always evident in what I would now call the rushing wind of the Spirit, which we can perceive in its effect on the reeds and in the sounds we hear. But as I read and re-read that scene from the children's classic, I knew that the whole mysterious love of God is encompassed in those events. The child that escapes to its freedom, is sheltered in the loving embrace of the god who has to be the demigod of the natural world of sheep needing their shepherd, the holy of holies where the strays can find rest and shelter, the loving embrace of the waiting father who rushes out to welcome his son back. Through it all is the invisible, ever-present power of the Spirit who comes as he is needed, and fades into the background when his job is done, to wait for the next moment of need.

Are we meant to forget moments of intense spiritual experience? Does not the psalmist tell us to 'Praise the Lord, O my soul, and forget not all his benefits'? (Ps.103.2). The Jewish nation relied on its memory of all the guidance and leading of their God through the wilderness years and the years of captivity. In that way, they were able to maintain their confidence that their God would continue to see them through to the future intended for them. And does our God want his people to forget Him, to let Him slip away into oblivion, so that He is remembered only as the saviour in moments of crisis or heightened awareness?

Saint Paul tells us that he is not dwelling on the past, even though he knows how much he owes to the saving experience on the Damascus road:

> Not that I have obtained all this, or have already been made perfect, but I press on to take hold of that for which Christ Jesus took hold of me. Brothers, I do not consider myself yet to have taken hold of it. But one thing I do, *forgetting what is behind* (author's italics) and straining towards what is ahead, I press on towards the goal to win the prize for which God has called me heavenwards in Christ Jesus (Phil. 3.12-14).

So Paul must put the past behind him, both his experience of rejecting the Christian teaching and persecuting Jesus' followers as well as his new life-changing conversion. He now has the presence of Christ in his life and that is a present reality, giving him confidence for the present and the future.

An overwhelming experience of the supernatural presence and love of God is the experience of many chosen by God. It is recorded that Moses experienced Him in the burning bush (Ex. 3) and Isaiah in his vision of the Lord on His throne (Isa. 6), and they had to press on with the task given to them. The dazzling experience propelled them, albeit reluctantly, into the service of God from which they could not look back. The vision could not last for ever; it would have been too strong to bear, the awe would have tired them out, robbed them of their acceptance of the normalities of daily living. God gives us our highs and lows, His Spirit comes and goes in differing degrees of intensity. We are granted the gift of forgetfulness in order not to be submerged under the weight of awareness without action. I had been exiled from belief partly because I had overlooked the mystery of belief in my desire for a permanent, heightened awareness and understanding. My early intense spiritual experience was something from which I had to learn and then move forward, having absorbed its wonders and benefits. It was not permanent and immutable. I had to recognise the mystery, be prepared to accept and let oblivion take over my experience so that I could simply live and enjoy the happiness of being one of God's creatures and loved by Him. That I did not realise in the spring of 1996 when I remembered my awakening that morning in Cambridge so many years previously and that, in my bewilderment and disillusionment, I thought had been merely an illusion making all my experience since then a mere trick of my imagination. I did not know that God was making me wait before revealing the mystery of a new faith to me. His Spirit like the wind blows in His own time and His own way.

This article was first published in *The Furrow*, Maynooth, Co. Kildare, May 2005.

Endnotes

1 Kenneth Grahame, *The Wind in the Willows* (Puffin Books, 1996). All references to this work will be given in brackets in the text.
2 Author's italics.
3 Kenneth Grahame, *Dream Days* (John Lane, Bodley Head, 1930), 59.

No Harbour?

A restless spirit's journey along the edge of belief, as reflected in works by W.G. Sebald and Franz Kafka

'What does it mean?',[1] is the question asked by W.G. Sebald at the end of the first chapter of *The Rings of Saturn* which I read soon after the collapse of my Christian convictions in the spring of 1996. I had been a Methodist local preacher for thirty-seven years and a house group leader for three decades in that time, but found my convictions evaporating gradually in the course of two months. My situation left me bewildered and confused. Eventually, after a period when I felt free to explore new realms, I started to miss the spiritual dimension in my life and decided that, as the Bible was temporarily or permanently closed to me, I would attempt to glean some reasons for my situation and some light for the future from a reading of other literature. Thus, during 1996, I discovered Sebald's *The Rings of Saturn* and found an immediate affinity with it.

Sebald was a free spirit who had emigrated from Germany to England in the mid 1960s, but had never felt entirely at home in England. His works defy categorisation. There is literary criticism (he was Professor of European Literature at the University of East Anglia), history, fiction and travelogues. His works have a meandering quality, but his meanderings conceal subtle thematic connections. *The Rings of Saturn*, published in 1995, spoke to me immediately as the product of his skirmishes with uncertainties and for his peregrinations along the fringe of society expressed in his book. I felt that I could join him in his explorations, yet in my search for answers remain uncommitted, justified and convinced by Sebald's own quizzical disengagement.

In his book a traveller, presumably Sebald himself, undertakes a journey through East Anglia, along the coast and inland, stopping frequently for conversations, reminiscences, digressions into historical events and diverse topics and personalities. The traveller visits country houses and once important coastal towns such as Lowestoft, overgrown parkland and dilapidated installations, and he visits the coastal village of Dunwich whose port is now sunk in the depths of history as coastal erosion took over. Virtually all the places visited have faded and declined.

The work is dominated by the theme of repeated patterns of growth, change and decay. Gradually it emerges from his apparently rambling account that history reveals a pattern of traditions and civilisations that have grown, flourished and declined, and that we in our present era are spectators of this decline. The journey along the periphery of the country, is in a cultural no-man's-land where civilisation is on the fringe of life and history. The traveller, and many of the characters he describes en route, are immersed in this peripheral world in which the subjects discussed do not form part of a new and growing civilisation, but remain rooted in the past. As I immersed myself in his account I shared the mixed feelings of melancholy and freedom to pursue fresh byways of thought and experience. But crucially I soon realised that my new freedom to follow his meanderings was taking me up blind alleys. My freedom to explore was being transformed by a sense of its limitations. Fascinating though the dead ends were, I wanted them to open out into new paths of faith. I found that God was using the dead ends and blind alleys to lead me along fresh ways away from the well-trodden main road of my former 'certainties', what John O'Donohue calls 'well-meaning, but dead names'.[2] I was coming to see that certainties are not faith, but that faith of necessity leads into the unknown and untried. I decided to explore Sebald's meanderings with new interest. I re-read his book several times and pursued the links that he made with other works.

The external link between subjects along his route is their obvious historical connection direct or indirect with the places he is visiting, often leading into lateral links with other subjects or places. The author is imposing a fictional pattern on the events, but it is not a narrative pattern that develops to a climax, except that the tour is completed. The book opens and closes with the figure of Sir Thomas Browne whose name recurs from time to time during the course of the account. At the start just seven pages into the book (9) Browne is mentioned as his skull is believed to be preserved in the museum of the Norfolk and Norwich Hospital, thus setting the tone for a constantly recurring series of references to death and decay throughout the work. On the last page (296), he appears again when, after a lengthy account of the growth and development of sericulture throughout history leading to its role in the history of Norwich, Browne is referred to as the son of a silk merchant, a fact not mentioned in the initial reference, but which rounds off the subsequent account of sericulture and enhances its significance throughout the book. For just as the worm produces the eggs which hatch, leading to growth through the larvae, then the caterpillar which in turn moults four times before the cocoon is formed, with the length of silk wrapped round the caterpillar to form the chrysalis, so societies and cultures grow, change and decay. In an earlier reference in the book, a Chinese Dowager Empress, Tz'u-hsi admires the creativity of her silkworms, a scene described as follows:

> Every day that came, Tz'u-hsi walked the airy halls [...]
> to inspect the progress of the work, and when night
> fell she particularly liked to sit alone amidst the frames,
> listening to the low, even, deeply soothing sound of
> the countless silkworms consuming the new mulberry
> foliage. These pale, almost transparent creatures, which
> would presently give their lives for the fine thread they

were spinning, she saw as her true loyal followers. To
her they seemed the ideal subjects, diligent in service,
ready to die, capable of multiplying vastly within a
short span of time (151).

The notion of dying in order to create and perpetuate new life is one
of the few tentative, half-hearted notes of optimism that offset the
pessimism pervading this work and one which caused me to wonder
whether the apparent death of my certainties might be the prelude
to an eventual reawakening. It is a note that abides in the memory
in the final words of the book following the mention of Sir Thomas
Browne's father as a silk merchant:

And Sir Thomas Browne [...] remarks [...] that in the
Holland of his time it was customary, in a home where
there had been a death, to drape black mourning
ribbons over all the mirrors and all canvasses depicting
landscapes or people or the fruits of the field, so that
the soul, as it left the body, would not be distracted on
its final journey, either by a reflection of itself or by a
last glimpse of the land now being lost for ever' (296).

The ultimate note is one of loss, of death, of an elegiac wistful regret
at the loss of 'the land now being lost for ever' which in the original
is *Heimat*, the German concept of one's native district that has meant
so much to the German consciousness throughout the ages. It is the
final thought in the book, the ultimate note that echoes all Sebald's
years of missing his country yet at the same time of wishing to be free
of the former associations that had alienated him in the first place, so
that 'his soul would not be distracted on its final journey.'

This theme still needs to be examined further however. At the end
of chapter one, Sebald describes Sir Thomas Browne's reaction to a
drinking glass which had been preserved from a Roman urn:

For Browne, things of this kind [...] are symbols of
the indestructibility of the human soul assured by

scripture, which the physician (Browne), firm though
he may be in his Christian faith, perhaps secretly
doubts. And since the heaviest stone that melancholy
can throw at a man is to tell him he is at the end of
his nature, Browne scrutinises that which escaped
annihilation for any sign of the mysterious capacity for
transmigration he has so often observed in caterpillars
and moths. That purple piece of silk he refers to, then,
in the urn of Patroclus - what does it mean? (26).

Amidst the enigma expressed in those final words of the chapter, an enigma that we attempt to unravel as we negotiate the maze of this book, Sebald makes his first allusion to a theme that is to resurface time and again in this account - that of recurrence through transmigration. A brief glance would tell us that this theme features constantly during the traveller's peregrinations. The journey has a beginning and an end, but within that framework there is an endlessly shifting pattern of recurring events, images and impressions, apart from the series of decayed towns, villages and country mansions many of which could be interchangeable. At one moment, on arrival at the home of his friend, the poet and translator, Michael Hamburger, the traveller Sebald has a distinct impression of having been in that very house and room in a previous existence (185). A little later in the same episode, he talks about an aged university lecturer, whom they had both got to know at the age of twenty-two, and twenty-two years apart, Hamburger in 1944 and Sebald in 1966 just after his arrival in England. He then goes on to say how frequently he experiences the feeling that the opinions he hears expressed in company have already been uttered with the same gestures and in the same words by the same people on previous occasions, as if he is a witness to a process of everlasting recurrence, what Nietzsche in *Also sprach Zarathustra* calls '*ewige Wiederkehr*' as the basis of his deep pessimism and what Sebald's traveller calls 'the ghosts of repetition that haunt me with ever greater frequency' (187).

Another major theme now emerges which reflects the fears I myself felt concerning the future in my new situation. Following the lengthy passage on sericulture in the final chapter of *The Rings of Saturn*, Sebald describes the presumed feelings of weavers working at their looms:

> That weavers in particular, together with scholars and writers with whom they had much in common, tended to suffer from melancholy and all the evils associated with it, is understandable, given the nature of their work, which forced them to sit bent over, day after day, straining to keep their eye on the complex patterns they created. It is difficult to imagine the depths of despair into which those can be driven who, even after the end of the working day, are engrossed in their intricate designs and who are pursued, into their dreams, by the feeling that they have got hold of the wrong thread (283).

Just as the silkworm dies in creating its thread, the artist like the weaver is imprisoned in his work and rendered anxious by the possibility, not only of the everlasting recurrence of unpalatable experience, but that this absorption might lead to his seizing the wrong thread and taking the wrong course. In an earlier work, *Vertigo*,[3] written in 1990, Sebald explores Franz Kafka's posthumous story, *Gracchus the Hunter*, an echo of which is detected in *The Rings of Saturn* at the moment just described and in the final sentence of the book.

In his story, Kafka, who had passed through Riva at the northern tip of Lake Garda in Italy in 1913, relates the arrival in Riva of a dead man who has been conveyed in a boat and is met by the mayor of the town. The dead man then comes to life as he lies on his bier and converses with the mayor who is expecting him to stay in Riva. When asked why he is still alive, the dead man who is Gracchus the hunter replies:

> My death boat went off course […] a moment's
> absence of mind on the part of the helmsman […] I
> only know […] that I stayed on earth and that ever
> since my boat has been sailing earthly waters. So, I
> who asked for nothing better than to live among my
> mountains, travel after my death through all the lands
> of the earth.'[4]

The initial mishap occurred while he was, like the weaver and the writer, doing his job, pursuing a chamois in the Black Forest when he fell into a chasm, was killed and was to be transported across the river of death. His final words, the closing words of this short story, are: 'My boat has no rudder, it is driven by the wind that blows in the nethermost regions of death.'[5]

The fear of taking a false irrevocable step is the ultimate anxiety expressed in Kafka's story and in Sebald's account of his journey through East Anglia. The notion of death in the moment of creativity is tarnished by the possibility of an endlessly repetitive recurring restless journey in which, as in the last words of *The Rings of Saturn*, a journey back to one's *Heimat*, one's home, is a distraction for the soul on its last journey.

My initial bewilderment at the loss of my Christian certainties was accompanied by alarm at what seemed to me to be the flight of all the birds that had been nesting and resting under my religious roof for decades. I then felt relief and found myself repeating to myself: 'At least you don't have to pretend any more.' I was not aware that I had been pretending belief, but I knew that I had been struggling with myself to maintain a semblance of conviction that my efforts towards goodness and peace of spirit had borne some fruit over the years. I realised, or at least I thought I realised, in March 1996 that my efforts had borne no fruit whatsoever, that I might as well admit the fact and that I could sit back and not worry any more, just be a human being with no pretensions and with the freedom to explore whatever ideas came my way.

As time passed, I knew deep within me that I needed a home, a spiritual haven in which my rudderless boat could drop anchor and rest. I had grown anxious that, while I had a good earthly home and good family relationships, my spirit was still bereft of any sense of direction and destination. I was growing older, soon to lose the defining role of my work that had served me faithfully for so long. I had never in my days of belief and in my preaching attached much importance to the life to come or to the fate of the soul after death. I had always felt that my preoccupations here and now, the tasks I had to fulfil were sufficient. Now that my boat appeared to have dragged its anchor and my spirit was drifting on the waters, I had started to grasp not for a firm theological conviction of a soul's heaven, but for a safe anchor, a home for my spirit which would be there when present associations had passed from sight. I was prepared for this to be a new faith, new faces, new convictions and hopes.

The hunter in Kafka's story was condemned to travel the world in perpetual limbo, in a state between life where he was active and striving and death in which he had nothing but regrets for a lost life and vitality. With all the love that I could share with my wife and family, with all the years of commitment to the spiritual dimension within me, I could think of no fate worse than being lost in a morass of uncertainty and unbelief, convinced only of the need to push my imperfect humanity towards some new satisfaction. I wanted eternal life, not eternal limbo. I wanted to return to belief.

God made me wait for a few more years. Now that my core belief in His presence has returned, I am still very much rooted in the present challenges, despite the invasion of memories both happy and painful and early morning uncertainties about the future. I just wanted, in my years adrift, to know that God was holding out a long lifeline for me to pick up and hold to, and that if for any reason I should miss or lose this chance, all was not lost and a fresh chance was offered to me.

Sebald was killed in a motoring accident in December 2001. In the summer before he died, I corresponded with him briefly on some of my findings from reading his work. When he died, I wrote to his widow to express my condolences. In her reply she enclosed a card with his photograph and the notice that he had been 'laid to rest' in St Andrew's churchyard at Framingham Earl, in Norfolk. On the front of the card were some words drawn from Ps. 91.4, written in German: 'He will cover you with his feathers, and under his wings you will rest.' The translation in the International Bible has 'find refuge', instead of 'rest'. It is the same, for his and all restless spirits a safe haven from the storm of restlessness, when Gracchus' boat will at last find an anchorage, where the endless cycle of recurring misery will be broken, our fears and uncertainties will cease and we will find rest in God.

This article was first published in *The Epworth Review*, October 2005.

Endnotes

1 W.G. Sebald, *The Rings of Saturn*, translated by Michael Hulse (The Harvill Press, 1999), 26. Hereafter all references to this work will be given as page numbers in brackets in the text.

2 John O'Donohue, *Eternal Echoes* (Bantam, 1998), 182.

3 W.G. Sebald, *Vertigo*, translated by Michael Hulse (The Harvill Press, 1999), 163ff.

4 Franz Kafka, *Gracchus the Hunter*, translated by Malcolm Pasley (Penguin 1979), 89.

5 Kafka, *Gracchus,* 90.

Waiting Beyond Waiting
Thoughts on 'unanswered' prayer as reflected in works by Franz Kafka and others

Two people are walking along a road from Jerusalem to a village called Emmaus. They are downcast when they meet a total stranger who walks along with them and asks them why they are sad. 'We had hoped …' is how they epitomise their frustration and disappointment that their expectations had not been fulfilled (Lk. 24.21).[1] They had waited a very long time for the Messiah to come.

In Franz Kafka's short, one-and-a-half page story *Before the Law*, which he wrote in 1914, a man comes from the country and tries to gain access to the Law. He is stopped by the doorkeeper who tells him he is not allowed in, but that if he does go through, he will be met by other doorkeepers each progressively more powerful than he. So the man decides to wait until permission to enter is given. The doorkeeper gives him a stool to sit on, and during the long wait, he asks the man desultory, unconnected questions about himself, while feeling increasingly that he must try to bribe the doorkeeper, his only obstacle, to let him in. As he grows older and death approaches, he summons enough strength to ask the doorkeeper one last question. He asks why if 'everyone is striving to gain access to the Law […] for so many years nobody but he has demanded to be allowed to enter'. The doorkeeper's answer is: 'Nobody else could gain admittance here, this entrance was meant only for you. I shall now go and close it.'[1]

The human race seems to have been waiting for answers to its questions since the beginning of time. We often feel we are destined to wait eternally. In the Scriptures there are according to my Concordance over fifty-five occasions when the question 'How long?' is uttered. The Israelites pined for answers when in slavery in Egypt and in exile in Babylon. They waited for a Messiah and had no idea when he would come. The world yearns and waits endlessly for peace. Nations wait sometimes patiently, sometimes in frustrated exasperation, for democracy to replace the arbitrary rule of dictators. People wait patiently and resignedly for new homes to be built after they have lost everything in floods, cyclones and tsunamis.

Christians often have difficulty in waiting for answers to prayer. Many abandon hope when prayers do not appear to be answered. Faithful Christians praying in faith often take comfort, when prayers seem to go unanswered, with assuring themselves that it is God's will. When, however, prayers for the healing of a friend or family member meet with a cure, they are convinced that God's will has been done. So convinced Christians find God's will in both types of response. A member of a house group that I led in the 1970s told us that she had been praying for her husband's conversion for thirty years. The fact that her husband, in his own words 'a card-carrying atheist' actually attended our group and made many perceptive contributions, was surely an answer to her prayer. When my beliefs deserted me in 1996 and I eventually began to long for their return, I found myself, with a sinking heart, realising that I might have to wait a lifetime, or indeed never see them return. I had to reckon on the possibility that, like Kafka's seeker after the law, the door might be closed for ever. And like Kafka's man, I decided that all I could do was wait and hope that my 'block' would be removed. But I am now prepared to admit that my very wish for restoration of what had been blocked out was the answer to my prayer which, because of my 'block', could only be expressed 'with groans that words cannot express' (Rom. 8.26).

Kafka later incorporated his story *Before the Law* into his novel, *The Trial*, published posthumously in 1925, in which Josef K is arrested one morning on a charge the nature of which he tries vainly to unravel throughout the story. He is torn between the natural desire to understand and remove the charge against him and the realisation that he must resign himself to his fate because the judges are not interested in the case, the outcome is inevitable and the investigation has barely begun anyway. In chapter 9, Josef K hears the story of *Before the Law* from a priest in an empty cathedral.[2] The priest comments at length on aspects of the story relevant to our theme. While Josef K is convinced that the doorkeeper is deceiving the seeker, the priest highlights the position of the doorkeeper himself. While it seems that the seeker is controlled by the doorkeeper, the latter is in fact subject to the presence and will of the seeker who keeps the attention of the doorkeeper fixed on him and refuses to give up and go away. The priest says: 'The man from the country is really free, he can go where he likes, it is only entry into the law which is denied him, and this only by one individual, the door-keeper. When he sits down on the stool to one side of the door and remains there his whole life long, this happens voluntarily, the narrative tells of no compulsion.' He goes on to state that 'the door-keeper on the other hand is tied to his post by his office […] He is in the service of the law, but he serves only for this entrance, so only for the man for whom alone this entrance is destined.'[3] Just a few lines later he summarises the doorkeeper's dilemma. 'The end of his service is […] determined by the end of the man's life, so he remains subordinate to him to the end.'[4]

Thus the interminable wait to which our seeker is subjected, but which of course he could avoid as the entrance remains open until the end, also imposes a similar long wait on the doorkeeper. The doorkeeper has to monitor his charge throughout, such that at one point when the man from the country, even though his sight is failing, sees the inextinguishable radiance coming from inside the door to the law, the doorkeeper, fixated as he is by the other man, fails to see it.[5] He is dominated by the nature of his task, to keep his charge under observation and maintain what he said at the outset – that he cannot allow him to go through that entrance.

Some points arise from this that bear particularly on our waiting for answers to our prayers or our heartfelt longings that we cannot formulate specifically as conventional prayers. These considerations need to be weighed carefully against each other. Firstly, while Josef K's freedom to abandon his quest is limited by the parameters of his position as an accused man, despite his being allowed to continue to work at the bank, and while he knows on the last day of his life that his executioners have been sent specifically for him,[6] we Christians are always at liberty to pray with persistent commitment and yet to continue our lives unimpeded, like Kafka's man, to get up and go away. Our waiting for answers takes its place amidst the normal run of our existence which, we hope, is enhanced by the patience that should be in evidence as we wait. Kafka's seeker however decides that his best policy is to wait until such time as he may enter. But, secondly, it may well strike us that our steady continuing with our normal existence lacks the persistence of the midnight caller recorded in Luke's Gospel when our Lord tells how he is rewarded with three loaves for his obstinacy and perseverance (Lk. 11.5-8). And the Canaanite woman, when her plea for her daughter to be healed is apparently refused the first time, persuades Jesus by her clever response of the degree of her faith and commitment to the cause of her daughter's healing (Mt. 15.21-28). It is possible that a single plea would not have achieved the result she craved, but persistence is needed.

So we have to balance patience with persistence. Yet, thirdly, our pleading and our persistent, single-minded waiting can become obsessive and impose excessive pressure on ourselves. In Friedrich Dürrenmatt's detective story *The Pledge*, the novel's protagonist, police inspector Matthäi, confronted by the grieving parents of a murdered child, makes the rash promise to catch the murderer at all costs.[7]

Because of the danger to all children he feels compelled to give up a promising career and spend the rest of his life in an obsessive fruitless waiting for the murderer to show his hand again, not allowing for the possibility that his promise might never be fulfilled. Our waiting has to be in hope rather than obsessive expectation of the fulfilment of our fondest wishes.

Donald Eadie, in his excellent book *Grain in Winter*, writes tellingly of his own wait for his serious back operation and conveys some lessons he had learned about waiting. He starts with the admission 'there is a waiting beyond waiting that tests the wanting'[8] and he sees that 'open-ended waiting is hard for us because we tend to wait for something very concrete, for something that we wish to have. We are full of wishes and our waiting easily gets entangled in those wishes [...] Instead, our waiting is a way of controlling the future. We want the future to go in a very specific direction and if this does not happen, we are disappointed and can even slip into despair.'[9] Later, Eadie, in his chapter 'Waiting for Healing', confesses: 'I have still not come to terms with my own deep need to control the timing of the healing process to fit my own pre-conceived programme.'[10] Our waiting is often overlaid by our hopes for the fulfilment of our agenda at all costs and we try to control God.

Thus, fourthly, our persistent demands for answers to our prayers and our waiting can mean that we put pressure not only on ourselves, leading to possible disappointment and even despair and abandonment of belief, but that, like Kafka's seeker after the law who pressurises the doorkeeper controlling him, we put such pressure on God that we start to bully him, rather than petition him and await his response. The puzzling, isolated instance when Jacob struggled with the angel and demanded a blessing from him may suggest the virtue of such perseverance (Gen. 32.22-30). Yet Jacob is retrospectively reprimanded by the prophet Hosea for his actions and told: 'But you must return to your God; maintain love and justice and wait for your God always' (Hos. 12.6). Much of the problem arises from a misinterpretation of Our Lord's recorded words: 'Ask and it will be given to you; seek and you will find; knock and the door will be opened to you' (Lk. 11.9-10). The feeling exists that we will receive a specific answer to our prayer, that we can, as it were, download an answer at the click of the mouse that is our prayer. If we look ahead at the words that follow in the Gospel, we read that a child asking a good father for a fish and an egg will not be given a snake and a scorpion (Lk. 11.11-13). It is clear that our prayers for good gifts will not be answered with evil and harmful ones, but that does not mean that we will necessarily receive the answer that we hope for or expect. We have to allow God to sift through our hopeful and expectant prayers and answer them as he feels is right and appropriate for us. Unfortunately, this might mean that the door that we want to go through is closed firmly. That again does not mean that another door will not be opened, a blessing that Kafka's seeker after the law is not granted.

I have already said that, when my beliefs deserted me, I faced the possibility that they might never return. I had by that stage wanted their return, but felt that my change from faith to confusion and bewilderment might preclude any recovery. However, in my inability to confront any doctrines or discussion, I decided to see if occasional glimpses of light could illuminate the murk and started to collect cards with short texts or brief thoughts that I could post around my room in the hope that some scrap of belief might return. That was my way of hoping to persuade God to restore my beliefs, while I realised that bullying him into a response would not help matters. A friend once reminded me that if you are stuck behind a long line of traffic on a motorway, it is useless to try to barge through, but sensible to try to go round on the outside and progress calmly, not forcefully. In fact, the loss of my beliefs meant that I had to wait, while doing what I reasonably could to show my commitment to the removal of my 'block'. My waiting had to be open-ended. I could not pray in the conventional sense, and I have always found conventional quiet prayer difficult. But perhaps my waiting and mixture of puzzlement and hope was enough. Mercifully, I did not have to wait longer than five or six years for my recovery to a new faith emerging from the embers of my experience.

At the time I could often see no way out of the impasse in which it was futile to struggle. A counsellor pointed out to me that my experience of alienation from belief probably resulted partly from the time in December 1991 when during my exchange teaching year in Regensburg our daughter, suffering from anorexia which reached its peak during her student year in another town in Bavaria, had been told frankly by a qualified person just a few hours previously in the presence of my wife and myself that she had every chance of dying before she reached the age of forty. That night, as my wife and I camped down on the floor of Caroline's attic room and I tried to cope with the realisation of what we had heard, I lay awake for hours, hoping to sleep the sleep of oblivion, but with my eyes fixed on the small skylight with the darkness gradually becoming greyer as the night hours edged forward. I wanted the darkness of sleep. I had to undergo total inner darkness with the gradual dawning of the new day no help at all. In the words that Thomas Merton uses for the title of a chapter in his writings I was undergoing the 'inner destitution'[11] of a broken spirit and only later did I appreciate his earlier words in his book 'Be empty and see that I am God'.[12] At the time the emptiness I felt in the long night hours when I simply wanted to forget and sleep in the hope that Caroline's illness would simply go away was not blessed with my consciously seeing God in the darkness. Even at that time my faith was severely tested. All I hoped for was that the new day might just possibly bring some momentary relief. My mind was benumbed and in total limbo. What Merton described as 'the serene darkness in which his light holds us absorbed'[13] only came when, some ten years later long after her recovery, Caroline was rushed into hospital with viral meningitis. I simply felt a deep resignation that, after what she had endured previously, she would not have the strength to survive this new blow, and in the mercy of God, at a time when I was just emerging from my period of 'exile' from belief I reached a point of serene and total acceptance of the worst that her new severe illness could bring her. Caroline, however, had different ideas and fought through with all the resources of inner strength that she had found in her from previously.

As soon as our waiting is overlaid by thoughts of fulfilment on our terms, it is not the waiting of faith which must be free of preconceptions whereby we mentally will God into accepting our expectations. Our minds must be like slates wiped clean for God to write on where we rest in the 'vivid darkness of God within us',[14] in the darkness between our prayers, whether spoken or uttered with 'groans that words cannot express' (Rom. 8.26), and the fulfilment of God's purpose for us. It is a waiting that is passive because it is bereft of our self-imposed expectations, yet active because we have put our trust in the hope of God's answer, whatever that answer might be.

Our formulated thoughts are by themselves imperfect. It is almost as if, in trying to shadow God, we are imposing our imperfect humanity on him. We have to heed the words of the psalmist, 'Be still, and know that I am God' (Ps. 46.10), words on which Merton based his own thought mentioned previously, 'Be empty and see that I am God'. We have to leave him to decide and be the sovereign God.

And yet we have still not confronted the possibility that the door may well be shut for ever on our prayers and our waiting without any apparent answer at all, that our waiting is simply ignored, or so it appears to us human beings with our restricted understanding. Ultimately, we must remind ourselves that our mortal feet are planted firmly on earth in the world of the visible, whereas 'faith is being [...] certain of what we do not see' (Heb. 11.1). But when the philosopher John Gray in the final sentence of one of his books, asks the rhetorical question: 'Can we not think of the aim of life as being simply to see?', is he not advocating a passive quietism which fails to respect our human desire for answers of some kind?[15]

But while we may not see the future, we have the assurance of past responses to our prayers and hopes, even if the responses seem to have been negative. While the Israelites were yearning for answers to their waiting, they could look back at what they saw as God's provision for them and their race over centuries. Kierkegaard, the Danish philosopher, says that 'like the one who rows a boat, I turn my back on my destination'.[16] A rower always has his back towards the direction in which he is rowing, so he has to fix his eyes on a guiding landmark on the shore behind him. He is also able to see very clearly the place he has just left. A Christian has the immense benefit of accumulated experience of blessings and answers to prayer, or perhaps of doors that have been closed to her despite her fervent wishes.

Sometimes we don't notice the answers to our prayers when they occur. In a short meditation, Ann Lewin compares prayer to waiting for the kingfisher to appear. 'All you can do is to be where he is likely to appear, and wait.' And often nothing much happens and there is no obvious sign, except 'the knowledge that he's been there and may come again'. You are prepared and you simply have to wait, until such time as 'you've almost stopped expecting it'. At that moment 'a flash of brightness gives encouragement'.[17] While Kafka's seeker after the law sees the radiance at the entrance when it comes to him, he attaches no significance to it because his eyes are fixed firmly on entering by that door.[18] His mind is closed to other possibilities.

A return to the final words of the doorkeeper will tell us that the door is meant for that seeker alone.[19] It is his destiny to wait, his frustration to bear. It is pointless being disappointed by not receiving an apparent answer to our demands when others seem to be having answers to theirs. In Elie Wiesel's short novel *Night*, Elie, recounting his childhood in Transylvania, tells of his frequent meetings with a Jewish teacher, Moshe the Beadle, who at one point speaks words that echo Kafka's: 'There are a thousand and one gates leading into the orchard of mystical truth. Every human being has his own gate. We must never make the mistake of wanting to enter the orchard by any gate but our own.'[20] We have often to look out into a void and see nothing, yet still trust that God loves and watches over us like a good father who may or may not grant our every wish, but who may well give us a flash of brightness to encourage us to continue waiting. But he may also keep us waiting beyond waiting and yet be answering us already in ways beyond our understanding. As Moshe says just a little earlier: 'Man questions and God answers. But we don't understand his answers. Because they come from the depths of the soul and they stay there until death. You will find the true answers [...] only within yourself!'[21] No matter how long we wait and look for outward signs, God's answers are ultimately waiting for us in the depths of our being and that is our entry through the door where we have waited and are perhaps still waiting for answers.

This article was first published in *The Epworth Review,* January 2009.

Endnotes

1 Franz Kafka, *Metamorphosis and Other Stories* (Penguin 2007, translated by Michael Hofmann), 197-198.

2 Franz Kafka, *The Trial* (Penguin 1994, translated by Idris Parry), 166-167.

3 Kafka, *Trial*, 170.

4 Kafka, *Trial*, 171.

5 Kafka, *Trial*, 171.

6 Kafka, *Trial*, 174.

7 Friedrich Dürrenmatt, *The Pledge*, translated from the German by Richard and Clara Winston (Penguin, 1964).

8 Donald Eadie, *Grain in Winter* (Epworth Press, 1999), 5.

9 Eadie, *Grain*, 6.

10 Eadie, *Grain*, 37.

11 Thomas Merton, *Seeds of Contemplation* (Anthony Clarke, 1972), 203-7.

12 Merton, *Seeds*, 178.

13 Merton, *Seeds*, 178.

14 Merton, *Seeds*, 179.

15 John Gray, *Straw Dogs: Thoughts on Humans and other Animals* (London: Granta Books, 2002), 199.

16 Søren Kierkegaard, *Johannes Climacus* (London: Serpent's Tail, 2001), 70.

17 Ann Lewin, 'Disclosure' from *Candles and Kingfishers* (Inspire, 2004).

18 See note 6 above.

19 Kafka, *Trial*, 167.

20 Elie Wiesel, *Night* (Penguin, 1981), 15.

21 Wiesel, *Night*, 15.

Part Two: Faith and Literature

A Bad Catholic?

Reflections on issues of faith and practice in Graham Greene's *The Heart of the Matter*[1]

'She's not a bad Catholic. She's lucky. She's free …' (217) are the words of Louise Scobie when describing Helen Rolt, the lover of her husband, Major Henry Scobie, the 50-year old Deputy Commissioner of Police in the unnamed West African state at the centre of events in Graham Greene's novel of 1948, *The Heart of the Matter*. While some of the issues in the novel are now seen through more liberal eyes, Louise Scobie's blinkered attitudes are still present in Christians of all persuasions, and the novel raises many questions concerning the dichotomy between legalism and true faith.

Scobie had fallen in love with Helen Rolt in the absence of his wife who had travelled to South Africa in an attempt to find a new lease on life after the weariness of her existence and the knowledge that her husband had been passed over for promotion to the Commissionership after his fifteen years of service in that country.

Louise attends mass and confession and her faith in Scobie's words is 'enough for both of us' (25). It appears that he became a Catholic in order to marry her and meet the requirements of her beliefs, but in the story he reveals much more knowledge of spiritual and biblical truth than most nominal believers, which suggests that he comes from a Christian tradition other than Catholic. Louise is very aware of his virtues. She says he has 'a terrible sense of responsibility' (79). Scobie is known for his scrupulous honesty and incorruptibility and Scobie's boss, the Commissioner, calls him 'Scobie the Just' (18). However, his great sense of responsibility and honesty are matched by a strong desire to avoid causing unhappiness and even to show pity, often in inappropriate situations. It is this latter tendency that undermines his professional standards and becomes his undoing, but the rot only starts to set in once Scobie has heard that he has been passed over for promotion to the post of Commissioner. It seems as if his will has finally snapped after so many years of probity.

The first indication of this comes when he fails to report that he found illicit correspondence between the captain of a Portuguese ship that had to be cleared to continue its journey and the man's daughter. It was a harmless letter, and Scobie tore it up out of sympathy for the man and because he knew that strict adherence to the rules would not serve any purpose in this particular case. He is compromised, but would certainly not have suffered professionally – after all he is only doing what is quite normal in that environment – but for his wife, Louise, who unwittingly draws him into his second and more dangerous step.

Scobie is unable to find the money to pay for her passage to South Africa and is reluctant to accept the offer of a loan from Yusef, a dubious entrepreneur, who has wanted to win Scobie's friendship and gain power over him. When Louise offers to abandon her scheme to leave for South Africa, realising that her husband cannot finance it, he is desperate to please her and takes up Yusef's offer. He only wants to make his wife happy! The loan is on a commercial basis, but he has taken money from a man of doubtful honesty and reputation and has played into his hands. The irony is that his wife has pushed him further along the road towards his doom. Without her pressure he would have probably ignored Yusef's offer and saved himself the later disastrous pressure that brought about his downfall.

Scobie, weakened, is now assailed by pity when, after his wife's departure, he at first befriends, then soon falls in love with Helen, the young 19-year-old widow who has survived the sinking of her ship. He is aware that he is committing adultery, but he manages, as far as he knows, to keep it secret. However, when Helen accuses him of being ashamed of their relationship, he writes a brief note to her to convince her of his love, openly confessing his feelings, which he then pushes under her door. The note falls into the wrong hands, those of Yusef, who is able to exploit the situation and increase his hold over Scobie. Scobie has been too weak to resist Helen's accusations. Pity and the desire to avoid creating unhappiness have again taken over. These human virtues, clearly out of step with his duty as a highly important and responsible member of the community, have led him into an acute awareness of his growing dereliction of his duty as a Catholic to shun adultery. He knows that he could not in all honesty go to confession and vow to avoid what he feels powerless to avoid – his regular meetings with Helen. And Yusef, in possession of his incriminating note to her, is now able to blackmail Scobie into handing over a secret packet to the Portuguese captain who has now returned. By now Scobie's dealings are becoming known to others and he is feeling that he has to lie increasingly, or at least withhold the whole truth.

On the return of his wife from South Africa, with her new resolve for them to start afresh and make their marriage work, Scobie is put under more pressure. Not only is he increasingly reluctant to give up Helen. Louise is pressing him to go with her to mass, and he tries to avoid this, finding excuses, but eventually having to accept the inevitable. So anxious is he to avoid hurting her that he cannot tell her directly of his love for the other woman. Louise, in fact, has been alerted to his new relationship and has come home for that reason. Such is her traditional love of her faith that she is pressing her husband to go to confession when she knows of the pressures on him. She must have a very strong belief in his sense of responsibility, especially now that Scobie is to be the new Commissioner after all and therefore all their ambitions can be fulfilled!

Scobie has no way out of his dilemma, except the for him impossible one of simply giving up his adulterous love for Helen, confessing and starting again with Louise whom he does not want to hurt, but for whom he can feel nothing more than a dutiful affection. So he starts to entertain the thought of suicide. This starts with feigned chest pains which he uses as a pretext for avoiding mass, but he begins to develop an elaborate strategy to signal the onset of a terminal illness. He feels that this is the only way of avoiding more pain for everyone. He has told Helen: 'I can't bear to see suffering. I cause it all the time. I want to get out, get out' (233). Later he says: 'I want to stop giving pain' (251), but Helen knows that all he wants is peace. He wants peace of mind, but without losing the life insurance for Louise, so his suicide has to appear as a genuine illness. He builds up a supply of tablets to take at one time and his diary entries reflect the developing 'illness'.

Suicide has already been signalled early in the novel. Scobie has had to attend to a young District Commissioner, Pemberton, lonely and heavily in debt, who has hanged himself. Scobie is aware that suicide is a mortal sin, the final act of despair that in the words of the priest, Father Clay, 'puts a man outside mercy' (86) even though the dead man wasn't a Catholic. When Scobie sees the note left by the dead man, he gently reproaches Father Clay, saying: 'You're not going to tell me there's anything unforgivable there' (89). While he knows that Pemberton was no Catholic and Scobie's orthodoxy tells him that the deceased is thus outside any condemnation, it is clear that Scobie has more liberal and forgiving attitudes and is only keeping to the Catholic beliefs by what he has accepted through his marriage and come to believe as necessary. Pemberton has signed his note 'Dicky', and in a dream soon afterwards, Scobie confuses this name with the name 'Ticky', Louise's term of endearment for him. Thus early in the novel, the seed is planted that will be watered in Scobie's crisis later. And as the idea takes root, Scobie finds himself justifying it when he says at one point that even Jesus, in his crucifixion, went voluntarily to his death and thus wished it on himself, a form of suicide. 'Christ had not been murdered – you couldn't murder God. Christ had killed himself: he had hung on the Cross as surely as Pemberton from the picture-rail' (190).

If we jump ahead a little to the time after Scobie's death when Father Rank in his conversation with Louise expresses the view that Scobie 'really loved God' (272), Louise still asserts: 'He certainly loved no one else' (272). She is convinced that her husband had been 'a bad Catholic' (271). Father Rank, indignant at her limited vision, tells her that the Church 'knows all the rules. But it doesn't know what goes on in a single human heart.' But ironically, even he, in his apparently enlightened attitude, in reply to her final words. 'He certainly loved no one else' reveals his own limited understanding when he says: 'And you may be in the right of it there too' (272). Father Rank having realised that only God knows the human heart, falls into her trap of judging Scobie without knowledge of his true feelings.

Louise has always believed that her husband didn't love her, despite his frequent weary protestations to the contrary. But while she may have been half aware that his love came from a sense of dutiful affection, she is more aware of his 'terrible sense of responsibility' (79) than of his instinctive compassion for suffering human beings, shown in his care for the dying child after the sinking of the ship, an instinctive compassion that soon leads him into confusing *agape* with *eros* when his relationship with Helen grows. What neither Louise nor Father Rank knows, are the final words that Scobie breathes as he dies: 'Dear God, I love…' (265). Father Rank senses that 'he really loved God' (272), but he doesn't know what the reader knows, that Scobie loves both God and people, possibly so much that he confuses love and pity and his love becomes weakness. Witness his reaction of love when he is standing over the corpse of his murdered servant Ali, but he has done little to prevent what he has sensed could happen to his servant at the hands of Yusef. He is incapable of tough love, the sort of love that Father Rank demands from him during confession when he tells him to cease his relationship with Helen.

The secret seems to lie in the quotation from the French Catholic poet, Charles Péguy, that precedes the opening of the novel: 'Le pécheur est au coeur même de chrétienté […] Nul n'est aussi compétent que le pécheur en matière de chrétienté. Nul, si ce n'est le saint.' (The sinner is at the very heart of Christianity. Nobody is as competent as the sinner in matters of Christianity. Nobody, except the saint.) Scobie, trapped in the sins of adultery and deceit and tortured by his over-active conscience, has reached the stage where he knows that he has sinned so much that there seems no point in trying to be saved. 'One may as well go on damning oneself until the end' (237). Why not go to communion and continue to commit adultery? Even the honesty that he showed earlier in refusing to repent and desist from what he knows he will continue to do has now evaporated. He now only wants nothing except that others should be happy, even if it means punishing and hurting God by his sin. He has despaired of himself for ever.

But a further look at Péguy's words show that the greatest sinner is the one who is liable to understand and feel God's mercy even more than the so-called righteous person. While this situation risks the charge implicit in Saint Paul's words 'shall we go on sinning so that grace may increase?' (Rom. 6.1), it is more than counterbalanced by Our Lord's words recorded in three of the gospels: 'It is not the healthy who need a doctor, but the sick' (Mt. 9.12, Mk 2.17, Lk. 5.31). While the believer should not trifle with sin, a believer who knows no sin or is so bound by conformity to ecclesiastical doctrine that (s)he has lost all awareness of personal failure or need of grace, is far from the Kingdom of God. As the priest in Greene's earlier novel *The Power and the Glory* muses: 'God might forgive cowardice and passion, but was it possible to forgive the habit of piety?'[2]

At one point in his rapidly growing despair, Scobie, having shown so much misplaced pity to others, asks himself: 'Am I really one of those whom people pity?' (202). The answer is that he could well be, but he is also one whom God loves, because Scobie has loved others, albeit confusing the nature of love and at the cost of his peace of mind and sense of professional responsibility. Greene's awareness that fatal human weakness and knowledge of the rules and demands of the Church dwell together in the souls of his Catholic protagonists finds its fulfilment in the honesty and sense of responsibility of the man in whom the virtue of pity becomes his undoing, but who nonetheless demonstrates tortuously the meaning of love and 'what goes on in a single human heart'. Unfortunately, he is not free to experience the joy that Saint Paul felt when he wrote 'When I am weak, then I am strong' (2 Cor. 12.10). But perhaps some saints are destined to remain locked in the misery of their flawed humanity unaware of the extent of the grace that only God sees in them.

This article was first published in *The Heythrop Journal,* January 2007.

Endnotes

1   Graham Greene, *The Heart of the Matter* (Penguin, 1971), first published by William Heinemann in 1948. All quotations from the novel will be given in brackets in the text.

2   Graham Greene, *The Power and the Glory* (Heinemann & Bodley Head, 1971), 202. The novel was first published in 1940.

A Bad Priest?

Reflections on regeneration in Graham Greene's novel *The Power and the Glory*

He is the priest who baptises a baby boy with a girl's name while he is drunk. This moment in the novel recorded on hearsay after the event is based on the scene which inspired the author when he was in Mexico, as he records in his 1971 introduction to the Heinemann edition of his novel first published in 1940.[1] In the novel the priest baptises the child with the name Brigitta, which happens to be the name of the child that he had fathered five years previously during a five-minute bout of drunken passion on a visit to one of the villages in Mexico. So he is a drunkard and has an illegitimate child. In orthodox terms and by any standards he can be considered a bad priest.

It is a time of great persecution of the Catholic church in southern Mexico. The bishop and almost all the priests have fled. Those who have remained are Padre José who has obeyed the revolutionaries' demand and got married, thus reneging on his duty of celibacy, and our priest who is never named and is throughout the novel simply designated as 'the priest'. He is on the run from the police whose lieutenant has sworn, out of a reluctant sense of devotion to duty, that he will take and shoot as a hostage one man from any village where the villagers harbour the priest. The story follows the priest in his attempt to escape capture and covers his dealings with various people who harbour or help him or who react to him in different ways.

But while he has grievously sinned, he is not unaware of his faults and is indeed highly sensitive not only to his situation as a hunted man, but to the sins and weaknesses that haunt him. Greene allows us to enter his thoughts and brings his character to life in an intensely personal way. But while the priest is sensitive and introspective, he is not always fair on himself. In fact, he suffers from poor self-esteem, and though his self-analysis is very unflattering, his actions, despite the obvious first impressions already mentioned, show him in a much better light than he is prepared to see in himself.

Our first encounter with him comes at a moment when he is attempting to escape from the country by boarding a ship only to yield to the entreaties of a child who asks him to attend to a sick person who is dying. While he knows that it will not help the dying person, the priest resigns himself to the fact that he is destined to remain in the country. Though his attitude is not one of gladly embracing his duty, he does at least respond to its call and stays. Later when the girl, Coral Fellows, who has sheltered him suggests that he could renounce his faith, a faith that she says she had given up when she was ten years old, he is appalled at the idea which he says is impossible. Throughout he is contrasted with Padre José who has capitulated and refuses all calls on his sense of duty, even at the end when the priest has been captured and asks for him to hear his confession.

Furthermore, on his return visit to the village where his wife and child are living he shows that he is prepared to die to avoid the death of any more hostages. The lieutenant has taken a young man as hostage after the villagers have refused to betray the priest. (No villager ever betrays him.) The priest, without directly identifying himself and without being recognised, such is his growth of beard since the early photographs were taken, offers himself instead of the young hostage on the grounds that he is now too old to be of any use labouring in the fields (90). However, the lieutenant refuses his offer, and the priest is free to continue.

While we never know his name, the priest when questioned gives the name 'Pedro Montez' (72), the name of the hostage who had been shot in a village recently. He uses the same name later when he is again arrested, not recognised and imprisoned overnight. The man Montez has died as a hostage and martyr in his place. A priest could be seen as an intermediary between the people and Almighty God, and Our Lord Jesus Christ, the Great High Priest, is recorded as having been the sacrifice, the scapegoat, for the sins of the people. But here, it is the citizen who is sacrificed for the priest, a role reversal which leaves the priest feeling even less worthy in the sight of God. Even then, the priest feels that it is his duty to stay in the country, even if everyone despises him and people are murdered in his place (74). He feels the dilemma very much at the time, and when he eventually escapes over the border, he is uneasy and feels out of place, as if, like the Bishop now living in Mexico City, he has abandoned the people.

While the priest is introspective and sensitive to his own failings, he is often blinded to the true nature of his feelings. One instance, for which I am indebted to Murray Roston in his excellent recent study of Greene's novels, concerns his attitude to his daughter.[2] Having fathered her, he feels guilty that he continues to love her and feels that he should not love the fruits of his guilty acts:

> He said, "I don't know how to repent". That was true: he had lost the faculty. He couldn't say to himself that he wished his sin had never existed, because the sin seemed to him now so unimportant and he loved the fruit of it. He needed a confessor to draw his mind slowly down the drab passages which led to grief and repentance (152).

The child is deliberately described as unattractive and objectionable in what she says to him, yet he is unable to hate her or forget her. After all, it is her name that he wrongly gives to the boy he baptises, such is the obsessive nature of his attachment to her. And after leaving her and his woman Maria in the village, he prays fervently 'O God, give me any kind of death – without contrition, in a state of sin – only save this child' (95).

The fact is that, whether or not the child is conceived sinfully, the act has taken place and the child now lives as a human being beloved of God. He has allowed his mistaken theology to blind him to the true state of his feelings, which are now of unfeigned love for her, now that lust has died. Despite his initial obvious sin in fathering an illegitimate child, in the words of the Apostle Peter, 'love covers over a multitude of sins' (1 Pet. 4. 8).

At one point he talks of the reasons why five years previously he had given way to 'despair – the unforgivable sin' (68). This echoes what Padre José has said about himself: 'He knew that he was in the grip of the unforgivable sin, despair' (54). This seems in both cases to be ecclesiastical or theological debris from better days when they both fulfilled the church's demands on them. It has the note of cliché, suggesting that both priests, who have failed their duty in different ways, are still unable to break away from the forms of thought and language to which they had become so accustomed.

Another way in which the priest is blinded to the true nature of his feelings, is in his comparison of himself with Padre José. While it is obvious to us that the latter has acted out of cowardice, our priest sees the other as the better man and himself as 'too ambitious' (111). Later in his conversation with the lieutenant after his arrest on his return from safety across the border he attributes his decision not to leave the country like the other priests to pride. 'Pride was at work all the time. Not love of God' (235). On the contrary, he appears to have an exaggerated sense of failure, highlighted by the presence of the obvious sins of failures in behaviour and priestly conduct that have clouded his sense of his true worth.

For he is very much an example of human frailty in a world that is fragile and weak. He has known all 'the sins that flesh is heir to', including debauchery, yielding to sexual temptation, dereliction of the exact letter of his duty, and despair. But he does exonerate himself on one crucial point, one that the author credits him with throughout. Once safe across the border, he muses: 'God might forgive cowardice and passion, but was it possible to forgive the habit of piety?' (202). When he is imprisoned and in conversation with the pious woman, he refutes her uncharitable comments about the behaviour of the couple making love in a corner of the cell and demonstrates his understanding of human sexual frailty. And clearly he is disillusioned with the easy life across the border with the Protestant missionaries. Piety is associated with the Bishop who has taken the easy way out, and the pious woman in the cell is to be released from prison shortly when her sister pays her fine.

The crucial point in the priest's favour and which confirms that he is far from being a bad priest, but one who is fully identified with the needs and fate of those he is bound to serve is his decision to return with the half-caste to give the last rites to the American gangster who is apparently dying and has desired confession. Incidentally, throughout the story the priest has always given confession to whoever has asked him, though often hurriedly and reluctantly. In this case, though reluctant and aware that his return will mean his betrayal by the half-caste into the hands of the police, he is convinced that the need is genuine when he sees the note from the American that the half-caste gives him: 'For Christ's sake, Father…' (215). So he returns to attend to the dying American, mirroring his very early decision not to leave the country by ship but to attend to the dying woman. Now, however, his decision is made positively, not reluctantly and resignedly. His desire to carry out his duty is enhanced by his realisation that to stay longer in the safety of his new surroundings would be against his deepest instincts and would be a concession to ease and comfort. He now knows full well that he is returning to his own arrest and certain death.

He had already encountered the half-caste who had attached himself to him on his trek to leave the country. Though detesting him and understanding his true nature, he had felt moments of compassion for him, betraying the fact that the priest, despite his awareness of sin within, has a full understanding that Jesus Christ came to save such as the half-caste:

> It was for this world that Christ died; the more evil
> you saw and heard about you, the greater glory lay
> around the death. It was too easy to die for what
> was good or beautiful, for home or children or for
> a civilisation – it needed a God to die for the half-
> hearted and the corrupt (114).

The priest has understood that his mission is to reflect that of Christ, to minister to and even die for those for whom Christ died, the corrupt, the depraved, even the pious. When he is arrested and taken back to be executed, he asks for Padre José to hear his confession, and when the latter refuses under pressure from the woman living with him, our priest confesses for himself without any priestly intermediary, indicating that he has to that extent severed himself from ecclesiastical custom and sought expiation in direct prayer to God. He has succeeded in his own mind in finding an independence of spirit free from the tradition he had inherited.

When he dies it is in a drunken state, the pain of death dulled by alcohol, true to his new self, grounded in his earthly fragile humanity, his death witnessed from afar by the dentist, Mr Tench, who happens to look out of his window and see the execution taking place in the prison yard. As the priest dies, he is seen to mouth a word that seems to be 'Excuse' (261). Is this the priest forgiving those who shoot him, or is he asking pardon for his sins? The matter is left open, but seeing that he has already confessed in the privacy of his cell, the Christ-like forgiveness of his executioners is a probable explanation.

But the impersonal detached nature of his death reminds one of the fact that the priest is never known by his name. It is as if he is a representative of his vocation, as if the vocation of priest is more important than the person fulfilling it, and that, although we know the thoughts and feelings of the man intimately, this vocation is ultimately fulfilled as His Lord would have wanted it. While the letter to the Hebrews, that great exposé of the mission of Christ as High Priest, tells us: 'For we do not have a high priest who is unable to sympathise with our weaknesses, but we have one who has been tempted in every way, just as we are – yet was without sin' (Heb. 4.15), we know that our priest is not the Lord, but is a mere human being, a shadow of his Master, frail and fragile, yet ultimately fulfilling his true vocation as representing his Lord and dying in full dedication to his calling, while demonstrating his humanity and imperfection. His death is contrasted with that of the priest called Juan in the story that the boy heard from his mother, a scene of execution paralleling the death of our priest, but expressed in conventional pious tones, emphasising the obviously saintly nature of the priest, Juan, in his death, without the human frailty demonstrated in the demise of our priest.

Yet the boy is instrumental in welcoming a new priest to the country, a priest who immediately gives his name. This signifies a new start, perhaps that the mission of the Catholic Church in that country has never finished and that all examples of martyrdom, whether the glorious one of the priest, Juan, or the inglorious death of our unnamed priest, can be used in the service of the survival and growth of the Christian faith under persecution.

In his conversation with the lieutenant after his arrest, our priest affirms his faith:

> God is love. I don't say the heart doesn't feel a taste of
> it, but what a taste. The smallest glass of love mixed
> with a pint pot of ditch-water. We wouldn't recognise

that love. It would be enough to scare us – God's love.
It set fire to a bush in the desert, didn't it, and smashed
open graves (240).

How can we assess the extent of our love, for God or for others? Or of His love for us and its effect? 'A little yeast works through the whole batch of dough' (1 Cor. 5.6), a point echoed in the same words in Paul's letter to the Galatians (Gal. 5.9). And that must be the justification for believing that this 'bad priest' may have found more favour in God's eyes than he is prepared to allow himself or many others to ascribe to him.

This article was first published in *The Heythrop Journal*, January 2010.

Endnotes

1   Graham Greene, *The Power and the Glory* (London: Heinemann, 1940), 27. All future references to this edition of the novel will be in brackets in the text.

2   Murray Roston, *Graham Greene's Narrative Strategies: A Study of the Major Novels* (Basingstoke: Macmillan Palgrave, 2006), 26.

There Your Heart Will Be
Thoughts on Covenant in the light of Peter Hobbs' novel *The Short Day Dying*[1]

He earnestly fulfils all his chapel and preaching duties. He posts tracts on the notice boards outside the local chapels. He trudges miles along empty country roads to keep his preaching appointments in almost empty chapels, and he visits the sick and the elderly. He attends the local preachers' meetings and enjoys the fellowship of other preachers. 'He' is Charles Wenmoth, a 27-year old Methodist local preacher 'on trial' in a remote circuit in south east Cornwall in 1870. But he is struggling to maintain his faith and enthusiasm in a situation where numbers and enthusiasm are diminishing.

Charles Wenmoth is the main character in Peter Hobbs' debut novel *The Short Day Dying*, written in 2005, a short work of fewer than 200 pages, written in the first person in a largely unpunctuated and direct diary form, recalling his experience in the course of one year in a harsh environment in which he knows little of the joy of his faith. He grieves for the sick, blind girl, Harriet French, whom he has been visiting and who dies during the story. His visits to her have assumed an importance very much greater than his other duty visits, and he is in fact in love, though he tells his friend James that he loves her 'in Christ'.[2] He works through the challenges of fulfilling what he sees as the responsibilities of discipleship to Christ, mostly called 'the Master', through illness, serious self-doubt and awareness of loss of belief, to an ultimate sense of new hope and a fresh start.

He is trapped in his present role, a role he has taken upon himself to the exclusion of the freedom he yearns for in the beautiful wild nature around him and that he enjoyed in his childhood to which he frequently longs to return. He had experienced an awakening four years previously and heard the call to preach two years later. But it is clear from the outset that he is relying largely on his own spiritual and physical strength, inheriting the preaching traditions of his father and grandfather and the inward and outward struggles of their tough rural existence in his new work as a trainee blacksmith once he had abandoned his work on the family farm just twelve miles away. He lives alone in lodgings, except for his very unfriendly landlady, whose attitude seriously affects his own outlook which is often judgemental of her and angry with the many neglectful and half-hearted church members and indifferent outsiders.

Charles' main problem is a life without any balance, highlighted by a much more balanced view of religion evident in his friend James and to some extent in his godfather, his mentor, who tells Charles 'I am a little worried for you'.[3] This imbalance is created by the 'weight of duty'[4] that he is bearing depriving him of the grace and joy mentioned much less, but which he could have been experiencing. In fact, at this time, Charles, regarding love as purely a matter of the will, is unable to experience the fullness of the benefits of God's Covenant offered to all Christians, tracked throughout Scripture and especially renewable for Methodists in the annual Covenant service (which strangely enough does not feature in this story) and yet found to be intimidating by many Methodists who either stay away from the Covenant service or participate in it with a heavy heart. My 'wilderness' period of five years in the 1990s was largely a consequence of a similar sense of personal failure to perform to the moral standards expected of me as a preacher and house group leader without any sense of the presence of God's grace to strengthen or rescue me.

So with an acute awareness of how I was eventually rescued from this, I wish to explore this balance in God's Covenant with us which I believe to be at the very heart of our Christian journey, without exploring interdenominational relations arising from the Anglican-Methodist Covenant which would require a separate study. Many of our fellow believers find that words in the Covenant service such as 'Put me to what you will', 'I am no longer my own but yours' and 'I freely and wholeheartedly yield all things to your pleasure and disposal' assume daunting proportions overshadowing the earlier words 'the power to do all these things is given to us in Christ who strengthens us' and 'trusting in his promises and relying on his grace'.[5] Perhaps for them the service places too much emphasis on what they perceive to be the superhuman demands of discipleship which, like Charles, they feel ultimately unable to fulfil. But the Covenant, so often referred to throughout the Scriptures, is given to us by God and starts with him.

Before the word 'Covenant' features in the translations of the Bible, the account of God's creation of humankind is immediately accompanied by the command 'Be fruitful' (Gen. 1.28). God creates and we are to respond to his command. Adam's freedom is conditional upon his obedience to the command of the Lord not to eat of the tree of knowledge of good and evil (Gen. 2.16-17). The first mention of 'Covenant' comes when Noah and his sons are enjoined to be faithful and fruitful in return for God's blessing: 'I establish my covenant with you. Never again will all life be cut off by the waters of a flood; never again will there be a flood to destroy the earth' (Gen. 9.11). This is renewed with Abraham who is told 'I will establish my covenant as an everlasting covenant between me and you and your descendants' and then 'you must keep my covenant', which he does in total obedience to go and occupy the land of Canaan (Gen. 17.7-9). When Moses is commanded to return to Pharaoh and speak for his people, he is given the assurance of God's presence (Exod. 3.12). When God gives, he asks and empowers, but he first gives.

When the Ten Commandments are given to Moses and God is laying down very specific tenets of behaviour, Moses reassures the people: 'Do not be afraid. God has come to test you, so that the fear of God will be with you to keep you from sinning' (Exod. 20.20). This is not sufficient to prevent them from falling away frequently, the 'fear of God' unable to shield them from the temptation to follow other gods. But though the punishment for disobedience is signalled (Lev. 26.15, Deut. 4.23), the mercy of God is always present to welcome his people back: 'For the Lord is a merciful God; he will not abandon you or destroy you or forget the covenant with your forefathers, which he confirmed to them by oath' (Deut. 4.31), reiterated after Moses' death, stressing again that God's covenant demands obedience and faithfulness (Judg. 2.1). The pattern of disobedience alternating with God's mercy and renewal of the covenant is demonstrated in Elijah's lament that the Israelites have rejected God's covenant (1 Kgs 19.10) followed by Josiah's renewal of the covenant 'to follow the Lord and keep his commands, regulations and decrees with all his heart and all his soul' (2 Chron. 34.31). The contrast between God's severity and his mercy is expressed many times in the Psalms, a clear example being: 'Their hearts were not loyal to him, they were not faithful to his covenant. Yet he was merciful; he forgave their iniquities and did not destroy them' (Ps. 78.37-38). In at least two psalms, the psalmist even demonstrates a covenant between God and the natural world of his creation, in which nature responds to God's loving creativity by bringing forth fruits of its labours and thus showing obedience to his will and love (Pss 104 and 148).

A major development is recorded when Jeremiah signals that the Law given to Moses is insufficient to meet the real needs of the people who are observing outward rules that are not embedded in their instinctive thinking and deepest wishes. But when he writes that in the new covenant the Lord says 'I will put my law into their minds and write it in their hearts' and that 'No longer will a man teach his neighbour or a man his brother, saying, "Know the Lord", because they will all know me' (Jer. 31.33-34), he is echoing what the Lord had already said to Samuel many centuries previously: 'Man looks at the outward appearance, but the Lord looks at the heart' (1 Sam. 16.7).Yet Jeremiah has previously stressed the severity of the Law in strong terms: 'Cursed is the man who does not obey the terms of this covenant' (Jer. 11.2). Even shortly after Jeremiah's new message is uttered, he reverts in his address to King Zedekiah to the former spirit of rejection of those who have violated the covenant (Jer. 34.18). But the seeds of the New Covenant to be fulfilled in Christ have been sown, and his new message that God has planted his word in our hearts is echoed in Isaiah in the words describing God's covenant with the people: 'My Spirit who is on you and my words that I have put into your mouth will not depart from your mouth' (Isa. 59.21). Earlier Isaiah has extended the covenant from obedience in personal conduct to taking God's message to the Gentiles, the blind and the captives (Isa. 42.6-7 and Isa. 49.8-10) and to all foreigners who have committed themselves to serve his God (Isa. 56.3-6). Such thoughts are opening up the covenant to all comers as Christians recognise this today. But such visions of the breadth and depth of love are often obscured by disobedience and rejection of the covenant and it is clear that the new spirit expressed in Jeremiah and Isaiah needs to be confirmed by the New Covenant in Christ which we now consider.

In the epistle to the Galatians, Paul maintains that God's promise to Abraham and the Law given '430 years later' are not in opposition to each other, but that the Law was given to fulfil the promise, to show our need of grace and to lead us to Christ. He continues conclusively. 'Now that faith has come, we are no longer under the supervision of the Law' (Gal. 3.15-26). That we are 'heirs of the […] covenant' fulfilling God's promise to Abraham is confirmed by Peter addressing the crowd in Solomon's Colonnade (Acts 3.25) and by Stephen speaking to the High Priest before he is stoned (Acts 7.8). And in the letter to the Romans, Paul shows how Abraham's obedience to God's call was a sign of God's grace to him as well as a sign that the

Law was being upheld (Rom. 3.31). However, 'a man is justified by faith apart from observing the Law' (Rom. 3.28). In the final analysis, grace supersedes the Law and the promise of God's presence and grace stands alone, superior to the obedience that is necessarily limited by our humanity and fallibility.

This is further confirmed in the letter to the Hebrews in which Jesus' ministry is stated 'as superior to theirs (the priests') as the covenant of which he is mediator is superior to the old one' (Heb. 8.6). The covenant under Moses was inadequate and had to be replaced by the one related by Jeremiah (Jer. 31) whose words the writer to the Hebrews quotes *verbatim* (Heb. 8.8-12). And the old covenant, enshrined in the Ark kept in the Holy Place and hidden behind the curtain in the Most Holy Place, was superseded by Christ, the new High Priest, who gave himself for our redemption by the offering, not of the blood of goats and bulls as under the Law, but by the gift of himself on the Cross (Heb. 9.1-14). 'For this reason Christ is the mediator of a new covenant, that those who are called may receive the promised eternal inheritance – now that he has died as a ransom to set them free from the sins committed under the first covenant' (Heb. 9.15).

It is clear, then, that our human endeavour to observe the injunctions of the Law and to live by obedience to a strict code of behaviour, labouring under the sense that the fulfilment of God's will and purpose depends on us and our efforts, is a misconception resulting in a one-sided and doomed attempt at religious observance. We have to recapture the sense that the Covenant has been given to us and is sustained by God in his grace, a truth that modern interpreters have expressed directly. G.K. Chesterton describes the essence of the faith expressed in the New Testament as 'a covenant with God which opened to men a clear deliverance'.[6] G.W.H. Lampe writes:

> It is not a matter of the favour of God being granted
> in answer to the observance on man's part of the divine

commandments. It is not the reward of obedience,
for righteousness, or a right relationship to God, is
no longer a state which man can attain by his own
will or effort. The new covenant rests simply on God's
acceptance of sinners.[7]

A little later, writing of the relationship between grace and obedience, Lampe refers to Zacchaeus' response to Jesus' call: 'Zacchaeus was not called upon to make restitution before Christ entered his home; he repented and made amends because Christ had already accepted him as a sinner' (Lk. 19.8-9).[8] In discussing Mark's Gospel in a recent article, Morna Hooker, while emphasising that Mark's intention was to 'persuade us to follow Jesus as disciples – and to remind us what discipleship means', states that Mark 'introduces his gospel as "the good news of Jesus Christ" '.[9] Discipleship comes from first hearing the Good News.

To return very briefly to Charles Wenmoth, he too had heard the Good News and his call to preach, but his discipleship had become his dominant motive, so that he has become a slave to his 'duties' and allowed them to weigh him down in frustration, anger and self-reproach. But the opposite too can happen. On the cover illustration of one of Nicholas Lash's books, Christ's disciples are depicted as being so sure of resting in the Gospel and love of Christ that they fall asleep in Gethsemane at the very moment when Christ needs them.[10] Simply basking in effortless quietism in God's grace without response is as unsatisfactory as a struggle for discipleship in one's own strength. A true covenant between us and God requires a balance of both acceptance of God's grace and our response to it.

A consideration of the gospels will confirm how essential is the balance between these two poles. In the Beatitudes Jesus' words 'Blessed are those who hunger and thirst for righteousness, for they will be filled' are a prime example of how grace and its influence through us are fused in one experience (Mt. 5.6). The fusion of obedience and the grace to live it is surely found in 'Remain in me and I will remain in you' (Jn 15.4).

But this still does not answer the nagging question how we fallible human beings can serve God without simply relying on our willpower. When Karl Barth says that 'God [...] is the initiator of the covenant', he is only confirming what we already know, that God acts before we respond.[11] However, when he speaks of our 'God-given freedom to obey',[12] and that 'God [...] determines human freedom',[13] is he not tipping the scales too far towards programming humanity's response, thus denying the meaning of 'freedom' as we understand it, a free-will act of our own choice? Surely we are no longer in his words 'a partner' with God,[14] but prisoners under benevolent constraint.

To find what I believe to be a true motive for a 'free' acceptance of God's will for us, we consider one parable that Jesus teaches. When Jesus is dining at the house of a Pharisee, a woman who 'had lived a sinful life' comes to overwhelm him with demonstrations of her devotion. When the Pharisee protests, Jesus tells him the following brief parable: 'Two men owed money to a certain money-lender. One owed him five hundred denarii, and the other fifty. Neither of them had the money to pay him back, so he cancelled the debts of both. Now which of them will love him more?' Simon replied: 'I suppose the one who had the bigger debt cancelled' (Lk. 7.41-43).

Jesus is saying that the greater the debt incurred and the greater the sense of debt, the greater will be the gratitude for the removal of the debt. The more a woman is forgiven, the more she will love the one who forgives her: our service is free if grounded firmly in a sense of debt forgiven. In that event, the desire to serve will be spontaneous, from love, because it springs from a heart overflowing with gratitude. This spontaneity arising from a powerful sense of debt forgiven enables us to show Christ's love, *agape,* to all, in situations in which we would not naturally feel love.

Another look at the Sermon on the Mount confirms this. 'Where your treasure is, there your heart will be also' (Mt. 6.19-21). Wherever and whatever our treasure is - material or professional success, domestic happiness, our hobby, or the service of God - it will take pride of place in our thinking and determine our actions. Our motivation springs from within us. Confirming the words spoken long ago to Samuel 'The Lord looks at the heart' (1 Sam. 16.7), in *Mister God, This is Anna*, we read much about the distinction between 'outward' and 'inward' made by the child Anna in her raw perceptiveness At one point her friend and mentor, Fynn, the author of the book, writes 'and God made man in his own image, not in shape, not in intelligence, [...] but in this total inwardness',[15] and the first words she speaks, in her spelling, are 'the diffrense from a person and an angel is easy. Most of an angel is on the inside and most of a person is on the outside.'[16] We are enjoined to love God firstly 'with all your heart' (Mk 12.30, Lk. 10.27). Jean-Pierre de Caussade, expresses the same thought as Anna, but in traditional eighteenth-century terms: 'God is only asking for your hearts. If you truly seek this treasure, this kingdom where God alone reigns, you will find it. Your heart, if it is totally surrendered to God, is itself that treasure.'[17] At the outset he prays 'that, by the habitual inclination of my heart, I may constantly repeat: "Thy will be done." '[18] He prays for the natural instinctive desire to do God's will in response to God's grace.

Charles Wenmoth is himself aware in his better moments that his faith must live in his heart rather than in his head and in the fulfilment of duties and discipline 'we come to know our Lord through what we see of the world, but only if the change is inside do we feel *him* there is a leap of reason and faith to be made and it is a wide chasm we must cross but then how happy and blessed are we to know him' (author's italics and punctuation).[19]

It may seem hard on Charles to say that his heart was primarily in his love for Harriet and that the illness and depression into which he sinks after his near drowning in the flooded river are largely due to his grief following her death. He admits this as he reviews his spiritual accounts later:

> But the reckoning of earthly matters has been quite
> tedious tonight and I have found myself longing for
> a system by which I might weigh up my spiritual
> accounts. I fear that my debts there are greater and
> swelling in number [...] I feel I have slept through
> the year not awoken from my soul's infatuations. Harr
> (Harriet) were the salt of the day and her company so
> sweet to me and because I have hungered for salvation
> I were drawn to her light and became so desirous of
> that perfect state that I lost my way.[20]

His lapse into grief, illness and depression manifests itself in a virtual rejection of the church institutions, meetings, preaching and visiting to which, in his adherence to his 'duties', he has become enslaved and which have now turned sour. In a better moment he admits that the nugget of his faith is still present, but his earlier desire for the freedom of nature and of his childhood has now become a desire to emigrate, to start afresh elsewhere.

But Charles has had to learn that freedom is not to be found in a yearning for the past or for a future life elsewhere, but in a free decision here and now. On his return to his family for Christmas having not seen them for a year he hears the Christmas Day sermon, which is recorded, but does not have any apparent effect on him. The text is: '*Behold now is the day of salvation*'.[21] As he sits in his room at New Year he sees that his notion of freedom has been misplaced:

> And yet I have felt free in the past so why not now.
> Each moment must be new. We have them briefly
> but they have not been lived before. Though they go
> quickly from us and there is nothing in the days that
> we have not already seen there must be room for us.
> Room for decisions and choices room enough for us

to be free so that we are not condemned to trudge
our plotted courses to their end without say on where
those roads lead us.[22]

In a recent interview Rowan Williams elegantly describes the balance
that marks the mature Christian life and which Charles is now feeling
his way towards:

> What you see is this balance, between dependence on
> the God who created you and that sense that grace and
> gift are utterly fundamental, and you rely on that. And,
> coming out of that, a certain authority in your own
> life, living to live your own life, and shape creatively
> your own life and the life of those around you.[23]

He speaks of freedom without specifying obedience, a freedom
springing from God's gift of grace and mercy to us allowing us to find
fulfilment in God's free service.

There is one final point to be made concerning the fact that
Charles, in his excessive worship of love for Harriet, realises that he
has lost his way. He now knows that the present moment is what
matters. Very many testimonies to their 'conversion' that Christians
give hark back to that moment of awakening, just as the Israelites
looked back at the Old Covenant that they had often broken. But the
best testimonies are those that say what God is doing for us *now*. Just
as at the beginning of time God created and empowered the world,
at the end of the Scriptures, God, the Alpha and Omega, recreates
us new and commands our obedience: 'I am making all things new
[…] Write this down, for these words are trustworthy and true' (Rev.
21.5). And Charles, who had missed his way and realised he was lost
would, because of his diehard Methodist tradition, only grudgingly
have admitted the truth of the words of the distinguished Catholic
theologian Nicolas Lash, referred to above, who tells us that God's
covenant with us which in his grace he initiates is saving us now
and giving us fresh grounds for free obedience: 'It is no part of the

Christian hope to fly in the face of the evidence and to deny that we are lost, badly lost […] Christian hope is sustained by the conviction which is received and cannot, with integrity, be constructed at will, that being lost, we are – nevertheless – being found.'[24] For, because in our weakness we have strayed, God taking on our flesh in Christ, with his heart of love, 'came to seek and to save what was lost' (Lk. 19.10), went to the Cross and was raised, redeeming us and sealing the Covenant on our behalf, for now and always.

This article was first published in *The Epworth Review,* March 2010.

Endnotes

1   Peter Hobbs, *The Short Day Dying* (Faber & Faber, 2005).

2   Hobbs, *Short Day*, 146.

3   Hobbs, *Short Day*, 95.

4   Hobbs, *Short Day*, 158.

5   The Methodist Worship Book (Peterborough: MPH, 1999), 288-290.

6   G.K. Chesterton, *The Defendant* (Dent, The Wayfarer's Library, 1901), 132.

7   G.W.H. Lampe, 'The Atonement: Law and Love' (from *Soundings: Essays Concerning Christian Understanding,* ed. by A. R. Vidler, Cambridge University Press, 1962), 176.

8   Lampe, 'Atonement', 190.

9   Morna Hooker, 'The Gospel of Mark' (from *Ichthus,* Vol. 158/4, Winter 2008), 4.

10 Nicholas Lash, *Seeing in the Dark* (DLT, 2005).

11 Karl Barth, *The Humanity of God* (Collins Fontana, 1967), 45.

12 Barth, *Humanity*, 79.

13 Barth, *Humanity*, 82.

14 Barth, *Humanity*, 76.

15 Fynn, *Mister God, This is Anna* (Collins Fount, 1974), 52-3.

16 Fynn, 13.

17 Jean-Pierre de Caussade, *The Sacrament of the Present Moment* translated by K. Muggeridge (Collins Fount, 1981), 46.

18 de Caussade, *Sacrament*, 6.

19 Hobbs, *Short Day*, 106.

20 Hobbs, *Short Day*, 195.

21 Hobbs, *Short Day*, 188 and 2 Cor. 6.2. Author's italics.

22 Hobbs, *Short Day*, 196-7. Author's italics.

23 Rowan Williams, interview with James Macintyre, *New Statesman*, 22 December 2008 – 9 January 2009, 29.

24 Nicholas Lash, *Seeing in the Dark*, 10.

Touching the Edge of His Cloak
Reflections on repentance and grace in Scripture and other literature

Repentance

In what is often considered the greatest of all parables, the Lost Son, away from home and living off scraps, repents of his folly and decides to return home. In another parable of two sons, Jesus tells of one who agrees to go to work in his father's vineyard, but then chooses not to, and the other who at first refuses to go to the vineyard, but then decides to obey his father's wishes (Mt. 21.28-31). Their father's reaction is not mentioned in either case.

The purpose of this study is to consider the relationship between repentance and grace, the extent to which repentance is necessary for the grace of forgiveness to be experienced and whether grace can simply be granted because of our human inability to experience true repentance.

The German theologian, Wolfhart Pannenberg, stresses the vital importance of repentance at the root of Christian experience when he says: 'Like John the Baptist, Jesus proclaimed the imminent Kingdom of God. This message [...] made turning back to God urgent business for them (his hearers) because the beginning of God's Lordship brings with it the decision for salvation or judgement.'[1] His assertion is such that repentance is made a pre-condition of all true Christian experience, but this underestimates the limitations of our human capacity to feel true repentance. Though it is true that John the Baptist came 'preaching a baptism of repentance for the forgiveness of sins' (Mk 1.4), experience of conversion to a life in the spirit can take a variety of forms and include a variety of different elements. The parable of the two sons in Matthew does not indicate any feeling of repentance, simply that the sons have changed their minds.

The parable is inserted in the scene in the temple when Our Lord is confronting the elders of the Church with their failure to act according to their pretensions. They have asked him by whose authority he does what he does. After his succinct parable he contrasts his hearers with the 'tax collectors and prostitutes' who will 'enter the Kingdom of Heaven ahead of you'. He then says that, while the elders refused to believe John, 'the tax collectors and the prostitutes did. And even after you saw this, you did not repent and believe him' (Mt. 21.32). The difference is again highlighted in the scene in Luke's gospel when a Pharisee and a tax collector, in the temple, demonstrate contrasting attitudes, the former praising himself and his own virtues before God, the latter confessing his sinfulness and need of forgiveness (Lk. 18.9-14).

In repentance, the fundamental need is for sincerity, which is difficult to assess. There is no guarantee that even the tax collector in the temple is sincere in his confession. How are we to gauge sincerity when all we hear are the words and perhaps a crestfallen downward look and a beating of the breast? But the context allows us to assume that the man is genuinely repentant. A return to the parable of the Lost Son and the Forgiving Father leaves me unconvinced of the complete sincerity of the prodigal's repentance when he 'came to his senses' and decides to return home. Henri Nouwen suggests that his repentance is 'a self-serving repentance that offers the possibility of survival'.[2] When the prodigal is recorded as saying: 'How many of my father's hired men have food to spare, and here I am starving to death. I will set out and go back to my father and say to him: "Father, I have sinned against heaven and against you. I am no longer worthy to be called your son: make me like one of your hired men" ' (Lk. 15.17-19), the impression is that he is acutely aware of what he has lost and what he sees others enjoying. According to Nouwen, the prodigal maintains that 'he remained his father's child'.[3] He compares his fate as the younger son deprived of his entitlements with the privileges enjoyed by his elder brother and even by his father's servants. And as Nouwen continues: 'He prepares a scenario'.[4] He is framing his change of heart accordingly. But, knowing that all our repentance bears the marks of our flawed humanity, at least he does sink his pride and turn back, and the point of the parable of course lies in the response of his father.

The biblical literature and the literature of fiction span the centuries in their penetration of the truth of human experience. While the Scriptures are limited in their composition to their time, their significance is eternal, and the writers to whom I will refer also span the ages in their understanding of the limitations of humanity grappling with a realisation of sin and its consequences. While fiction may traditionally have been seen as far from biblical truth, Our Lord himself in his ministry taught through stories demonstrating the deep truths of human experience and God's love. And even writers sceptical of faith may be used in God's purposes to convey the truths of the Scriptures unconsciously. For Christian readers of fiction, and those of other faiths or none, truths are only in the texts when we find them. It has been said that 'the truth is never simply and objectively resident in a text; rather it is found in the interaction between text and reader.'[5] The discovered truth has to be grasped and assimilated by each of us before it becomes our truth. Both types of literature may be considered in their context in tandem as representing differing aspects of the relationship between repentance and grace.

Sophocles

It is indeed possible to convince oneself that one has made a full and complete act of repentance while withholding elements of the truth about one's experience. While the Greek tragedians constantly demonstrate the enormous guilt of their protagonists, true repentance or in some cases, any form of repentance is prevented by the fact that guilt is often ascribed to the force of an inscrutable fate guiding their hand. For instance, in Sophocles' *King Oedipus,* Oedipus in his dialogue with Jocasta accepts his guilt for the murder of his father, Laius, in an outpouring of penitence for his crime:

> Is there any more wretched mortal than I, more hated
> By God and man?

And just two lines later:

> On me is the curse that none but I have laid.

But he immediately transfers the blame on to the gods:

> Can it be any but some monstrous god
> Of evil that has sent this doom upon me?[6]

His acceptance of guilt and his genuine sorrow at his actions are tempered in his own mind by the possibility that he is predestined by some power greater than himself to commit patricide. However, in the third part of the trilogy, *Antigone,* Creon, bringing in the corpse of his son, Haemon, in the final scene, admits his full responsibility for the death of both his son and Antigone:

> Behold the slayer, the slain,
> The father, the son,
> O the curse of my stubborn will![7]

But he has no time in the remaining moments of the play to make amends, and has to live on in his despair and loneliness. But his admission of responsibility is a confession of his guilt without any attempt to excuse or exonerate himself.

The Old Testament

In the Old Testament we find that King David also freely confesses his guilt:

> Wash away all my iniquity
> And cleanse me from my sin.
> For I know my transgressions
> And my sin is always before me.
> Against you, you only, have I sinned
> And done evil in your sight (Ps. 51.2-4).

He makes no excuses, but it is guilt arising from a totally different source from Creon's. David is an obvious instance of a man who has yielded to his natural human impulses in his lust for Bathsheba, but has sinned even further in contriving to have her husband, Uriah, sent out to die in the front line, so that he, David, can enjoy her. He has acted shamefully because of his initial lust. His abject repentance is expressed openly and primarily in this psalm. And he goes on to confess that he was

> Sinful at birth,
> Sinful from the time my mother conceived me (v. 5).

His prayer is for a complete cleansing and a restoration of joy, as a consequence of which he will act to serve God and praise His name:

> Then I will teach transgressors your ways,
> And sinners will turn back to you (v. 13).

David is an obvious example of repentance issuing in a full transformation of his life, though in his confession in Psalm 51 he omits any reference to the harm he has done to his fellow human beings, in particular Uriah, and one could therefore suggest that his repentance falls short in that respect. Cain however, notorious as the slayer of his brother, is a different case. In Genesis 4, we learn that God has given preference to his brother Abel, apparently as Cain, a tiller of the soil, has produced less obvious fruits of his labours than his brother who, tending his flocks, has 'brought fat portions from some of the firstborn of his flock'. We see that 'the Lord looked with favour on Abel and his offering, but on Cain and his offering he did not look with favour' (Gen. 4.4-5). Whatever the Lord's preference, Cain's fratricide is clearly inexcusable. Like Adam and Eve, who deny their responsibility, with Adam blaming Eve and Eve blaming the serpent for their lapse into disobedience, Cain has also rejected any responsibility for his brother's fate saying: 'Am I my brother's keeper?' (Gen. 4.9). However, when the Lord spells out the punishment for his crime, the curse of the unfruitful soil that Cain will be working from now on and that he will wander the earth, he is smitten with remorse. Cain's reaction is in complete contrast to what has gone before:

> 'Cain said to the Lord, "My punishment is more than I
> can bear. Today you are driving me from the land, and
> I will be hidden from your presence; I will be a restless
> wanderer on the earth, and whoever finds me will kill
> me" ' (vv. 13-14).

His reaction is a mixture of self-pity for what he will have to endure as an outcast exposed to the possibility of being murdered himself and deep regret that he will no longer know the presence of God who will be hidden from him. Henri Blocher writes that Cain 'commiserates with himself and utters not a word of regret for the act he has committed'.[8] However, the Lord's response is to place a mark of protection on him so that 'if anyone kills Cain, he will suffer vengeance seven times over' (Gen. 4.15). While Cain is still subject to the curse and remains an outcast, arguably so that he is constantly reminded of the consequences of his acts, he at least has the Lord's protection, as Gerhard von Rad says: 'Cain does not have the last word in this story, but rather God, who now places Cain's forfeited life under strict protection [...] Because of his murder he is cursed by separation from God and yet incomprehensibly guarded and supported by God's protection.'[9] It is a measure of God's acceptance, that ultimately He cannot abandon Cain even though he has only expressed a limited form of repentance for his crime.

Moses presents a totally different case. He had killed the Egyptian overseer and fled into the wilderness. When he is confronted by God's call from the burning bush, he is terrified and admits his total unsuitability for the Lord's work in the words:

> 'Who am I, that I should go to Pharaoh and bring the Israelites out of Egypt?' (Exod. 3.11).

He queries the purpose and wisdom of the Lord's commands and asks to be spared the onerous duties now placed upon him. But there is no record that he actually repents of any past deed. He is simply told that God, who is the God of Abraham, Isaac and Jacob, will equip him for the task that is required of him. However, Isaiah, called to the service of God, is filled with an overwhelming sense of wonder at the vision he sees in the temple (Isa. 6). He too, like Moses, is full of the sense of his own unworthiness and unsuitability for the commission that the Lord has entrusted to him. The difference is that Isaiah experiences the lifting of his guilt and the atonement of his sin, and his acceptance of the commission is swifter than Moses' who questions God more before accepting his new role.

Saint Paul

This brings us to the moment of Saul's conversion on the road to Damascus. This event demonstrates that the transformation of life is not immediately prefaced by a direct realisation of sin. We know relatively little of Paul before the event. At the end of Acts chapter 7, we read that he is present at the death of Stephen, and the implication is that he is subconsciously impressed by the saintliness that Stephen shows in his death when Stephen, like Christ, forgives those who have stoned him to death (Acts 7.60). Chapter 8 contains the account of his persecution of the Christians. Then his dramatic conversion takes place. Blinded by an overwhelmingly dazzling light, he hears the voice of God asking why he is persecuting Him, the Lord. He is not directly constrained to repent, but is so dazzled by the transcendent glory of the divine presence and so totally dependent on the Lord restoring his sight to him that a realisation of his need and total dependence on God take place. Sometimes God convicts by the sheer dazzling brilliance and wonder of His glory and shakes us by the total contrast between that and our human limitations. Saul's dependence on God is demonstrated by his immediate response to God as 'Lord', even though he must have been mystified by the event that had happened. But he knows that as God challenges him to say why he is persecuting *Him*, it is the Lord who is speaking. The conversion and repentance are total, confirmed by his baptism, reconciliation with the other disciples and by his immediate preaching of the Gospel, resulting in his missionary zeal and total commitment. When he refers several times to his initial encounter with Christ in the words: 'Have I not seen Jesus our Lord?' (1 Cor. 9.1), it is not to dwell on the dramatic details of his conversion as an isolated event (1 Cor. 15.8), but to say that the gospel came 'by revelation from Jesus Christ' (Gal. 1.12), that 'God was pleased […] to reveal his Son in me' (Gal. 1.16) and that he sees the 'light of the knowledge of the glory of God in the face of Christ' (2 Cor. 4.6). However, as his experience of the grace and love of God grows, Paul confesses his own constant need to repent of his inability to do what his good intentions direct him to and his constant failure to resist the evil that he knows he should resist (Rom. 7.15-19). He continues: 'What a wretched man I am! Who will rescue me from this body of death? Thanks be to God – through Jesus Christ our Lord!' (Rom. 7.24-25). He who has received such life-changing grace is aware of the human nature from which he has been saved and of his constant tendency to fall into sin. This has become his concern, relegating references to his previous experience before conversion to two passages (Gal. 1.13-15 and Phil. 3.5-9) primarily as a matter of comparison.

What is clear from the words and experience of Paul is that an initial act of repentance and turning to God needs constantly to be supplemented by an awareness of our daily inadequacy in living up to the call of the Spirit within us and our failure to follow the commands and standards that Christ Jesus has set us. In the scene in the upper room during the Last Supper, Simon Peter makes the mistake of assuming that if he has to be cleansed he has to have not only his feet, but his hands and his head washed by Jesus as well. Our Lord says: 'A person who has had a bath needs only to wash his feet; his whole body is clean' (Jn 13.10). We have already experienced what we may call 'primary washing' as an act of repentance, but we do need a 'secondary washing', forgiveness for our daily failings in worship, love and service, just as the early disciples had to wash the dust from their bare feet after a day on the road. Later, Jesus says to his disciples: 'You are already clean because of the word I have spoken to you' (Jn 15.3), but as branches of himself, the Vine, they have to be pruned. Many Christians do themselves a spiritual disservice by their constant feeling that their life is a fundamental and everlasting state of penitence which can deprive them of joy in their salvation.

It has emerged, therefore, that the moment of turning to respond to God is not always accompanied by an act of true repentance, but by some other reaction, either the sense of being overwhelmed by the glory of God or by a moment of realisation of our human limitations.

Thomas Hardy

As we have seen, realisation of our need does not automatically lead to confession and the acceptance of forgiveness. At this point we should turn to consider the experience of Thomas Hardy's Mayor of Casterbridge who knows his catastrophic failings and repents of them, but does not experience grace or peace.

Michael Henchard is fatally impulsive and bitterly regrets the acts in his past towards his family which eclipse the goodness he has shown towards the community he has served: 'Why should I still be subject to these visitations of the devil, when I try so hard to keep him away?'[10] In true Hardy fashion, he sees himself as the victim of powerful forces of fate embodied in his personal devil who dogs his steps throughout his life. When he dies a piece of paper is found on his body stating his will. Among other things, he wants simply to be forgotten and for nobody to grieve over him.[11] He is saved from suicide and taken home. However, his words 'Who is such a reprobate as I! And yet it seems that even I be in Somebody's hand'[12] indicate his awareness of a guiding supernatural power in his life. Despite his feeling of total worthlessness, he has recently helped the mother of a local man, Abel Whittle, who in return has followed him to tend him in his final illness. He is so unaware of the extent of the goodness he has shown in his life that, as he is dying, he asks Whittle: 'Can ye be really such a poor fond fool as to care for such a wretch as I?'[13]

Hardy's bleak sense that man is dogged by an inscrutable fate means that his character achieves a miserable self-awareness and regret which still leaves him in a quagmire of futile self-reproach with no ability to forgive himself and move on into a state of joy. Circumstances do not seem to allow him the regeneration he desires and needs. Yet the Christian reader would glimpse possibilities that Henchard is only half aware of. He has an undeveloped, half understood sense of a divine presence in his life, if only when it is too late for him to enjoy it. His position is an extreme form of the everlasting penitence that some feel who are aware of their frailty and mentally repent of it constantly, but are incapable of finding freedom from its power. Henchard, like many others, would be unable to share the thoughts of John O'Donohue in his wonderful book *Eternal Echoes*, who says:

> When personal guilt in relation to a past event
> becomes a continuous cloud over your life, then you
> are locked in a mental prison [...] While you should
> not erase your responsibility for the past, when you
> make the past your jailer, you destroy your future. It is
> such a great moment of liberation when you learn to
> forgive yourself, let the burden go and walk out into a
> new path of promise and possibility.[14]

Realisation of personal sin without freedom from self-loathing leaves the sensitive individual in a worse emotional state than no self-awareness at all. And Judas Iscariot who has known the presence of Christ in his life knows repentance and self-disgust without seeking the forgiveness of the One he has betrayed and without ever feeling that he would be justified in ever being forgiven.

Thus, both realisation of sin and repentance exist in differing forms and to a different extent. Awareness of personal guilt is often present without repentance, and there may be conversion and transformation without an obvious act of penitence, purely through the force of the dazzling light of God's glory that shines on the unreformed life and makes us aware of past errors and new possibilities. Self-knowledge is necessary in the total Christian experience, even if it first happens during the development of a deepening relationship with Christ as Saviour. Paul certainly knows what he has to repent of once he has seen God's glory. There is surely no required sequence in the Christian's developing experience. But we now need to consider in greater detail the gift of forgiveness which eludes so many who experience incomplete self-knowledge and repentance.

Grace and forgiveness

There is a moment recorded in the ministry of Jesus when a woman who had been 'subject to bleeding for twelve years' but is unable to attract Jesus' attention, tells herself: 'If I only touch his cloak, I will be healed' (Mt. 9.20-21). This recurs later when, after Jesus has landed at Gennesaret, he is recognised by the people and they bring their sick to him, begging him 'to let the sick just touch the edge of his cloak, and all who touched him were healed' (Mt.14.36). It is their last desperate act of faith that Jesus will be able to accomplish the virtually impossible, the conviction that in our powerlessness all we can do is throw ourselves on his healing grace and trust that he can do what we are incapable of achieving for ourselves. While these instances are not directly moments of repentance, it is also clear that Jesus sees physical disease as symptomatic of unforgiven sin, an instance of this being the occasion when, after the healing of the invalid at the pool of Bethesda, Jesus sees him later and tells him: 'Stop sinning, or worse may happen to you' (Jn 5.14). A classic instance of the same is the moment when the paralytic man is lowered down through the open roof into the presence of Jesus by friends who, like the woman who touches the edge of his cloak, are unable to reach Jesus because of the crowds of people wanting to see him. The first thing that Jesus says to him is: 'Son, your sins are forgiven' (Mt. 2.5). Pannenberg writes: 'Like the promise of forgiveness and the assurance of salvation, so too Jesus' healing ministry was closely bound up with his message of the coming of the Kingdom of God. The healing he performed demonstrated concretely that where the message of God's nearness is grasped completely and in full trust, salvation itself is already effective.'[15] It is highly unlikely that any of the three have any awareness of the need to repent or of unconfessed and unforgiven sin. The emphasis has shifted from the personal consciousness of inward and spiritual need to the actions of the One who acts to help us despite our limitations, our ignorance and our moral blindness. In the parable of the Lost Son, it is the spontaneous forgiveness of the Father that matters, rather than the reactions of the prodigal. We are in the realm of grace.

When Jesus pronounces his forgiveness from the Cross, who is He forgiving? While he says 'Forgive *them*' (Lk. 23.34),[16] is he only forgiving those who are his immediate executioners? He is surely including Judas among them, and the disciples who flee from him at the moment of his arrest. And surely he is looking ahead at Simon Peter who also betrays Him, but who unlike Judas has the immense benefit of Jesus' forgiveness and recommissioning. Simon Peter repents bitterly and weeps, but do the authorities, Pontius Pilate and the High Priest, also feel any repentance for their actions? While Jesus from the Cross allows for the fact that 'they do not know what they are doing' (Lk. 23.34), His vision is, however, that while they know the immediate consequences of their acts, they are unaware of their deeper significance – that they have followed God's plan that He should suffer and bring redemption to the world, past, present and future without any repentance or understanding of the consequences.

Even those who died in faith in God before Christ was born are justified for their belief. Paul sees this in his reference to Abraham when he reiterates the reference to God's covenant with him (Gen. 15.6) and reaffirms in the original words from Genesis 'Abraham believed God, and it was credited to him as righteousness' (Rom. 4.3). The promise of grace is given to Abraham and his descendants on the basis of their faith alone. This is also promised to David who certainly knows repentance and craves forgiveness when, in the same passage, Paul repeats the words of Ps. 32.1-2:

> Blessed are they
> whose transgressions are forgiven,
> whose sins are covered.
> Blessed is the man
> Whose sin the Lord will never count against him
> (Rom. 4.7-8).

Abraham's faith is not yet the towering faith and obedience recorded in his readiness to sacrifice Isaac. The faith can be as 'small as a grain of mustard seed' (Mt. 17.20 and Lk. 17.6). Who is to assess the size and extent of the faith required? It can indeed be the faith of the woman who simply wants to touch 'the edge of his cloak' (Mt. 9.20).

And just as in the mind of the immortal God, creator of Time, who spans the ages and sees the lives of humanity as one moment, the faith of past generations is accepted, the promise is also to us, the present-day disciples who, like Peter and the others, have time and again fled from Him and denied Him. And when Pontius Pilate washes his hands and says: 'I am innocent of this man's blood' and the crowd responds with the words: 'Let his blood be on us and on our children!' (Mt. 27.24-25), it is not only the Jewish crowd who will bear responsibility, but all those present and future whose actions, neglect and failure have added or will add to His death. 'All have sinned and fall short of the glory of God' writes Paul (Rom. 3.23), and still do fall short, as Paul has just written: 'This righteousness from God comes through faith in Jesus Christ to all who believe. There is no difference' (Rom. 3.22). All stand under the same judgement and have access to the same promise of justification and acceptance in His sight. And lest we place too much emphasis on our own virtue in the faith we have, Tom Wright reminds us where the true virtue lies: 'When God's covenant faithfulness/justice is unveiled, this is done *on the basis of the faithfulness of Jesus the Messiah*, on the one hand, and *for the benefit of those who believe* on the other.'[17] We are justified by God's grace for our faith. The grace of God covers the sins and failures of all humanity and all ages because God knows the frail humanity of those He has created and knows that His Grace and strength are made perfect even if our realisation of our weakness and our repentance fall so far short.

It is emerging from our reflections that, while our concentration so far has been on individual cases and on the repentance of the individual, the offer of forgiveness on the basis of faith alone is a collective offer to all. It is important at this point to consider that, while the entire human race is included in the grace that is extended to us, the whole of humanity is called to repentance.

Collective Repentance

When John the Baptist comes 'preaching a baptism of repentance for the forgiveness of sins' (Mk 1.4) he comes not only to challenge individuals, but the entire nation of Israel. Jesus' judgement on the Pharisees and the ecclesiastical authorities and the parable of the wedding feast (Mt. 22.1-13), telling of the privileged guests' rejection of the invitation to the banquet and the consequent invitation to the outsiders to take their place at the feast, are indications of Our Lord's opening up his mission to races other than the nation of Israel. But the disease of rejection of Christ and the failure to repent spreads throughout the rest of humanity and history into our own day, such that history falls under the same judgement of having failed to follow and obey the commands of God or even to accept the moral precepts of the Ten Commandments. Surely, while many may reject the authority of God as Lord of the universe and see no relevance in the first of Jesus' two great commandments, there is no reason why human beings should reject the second commandment: 'Love your neighbour as yourself' (Mk 12.30-31). Acceptance of the relevance of the second commandment is surely not conditional on acceptance of a belief in God's authority over our lives: it is the creed of all who seek to live in harmony with their fellow beings and further the good of the human race. It is therefore important to accept that the entire human race is in need of repentance for its neglect of the interests of our fellow beings, our planet, our environment and the resources of the world that are being abused and wasted. It has very often been the case that confessing Christians have been less aware of their failings than non-believers observing them. Many professing belief and goodwill suffer from a form of wilful blindness, by which it is easy to convince oneself that what is happening is not happening at all.[18] When Jesus on the Cross forgives the world, it is not only for our actions in crucifying Him, but in crucifying our disadvantaged fellow human beings who are crying out for our help and love. An important aspect of our imperfect repentance is that we as Christians, throughout history, have collectively failed to speak out and act firmly enough to reverse the harm that is happening, while at the same time we are perhaps acting as individuals within our human limits to alleviate suffering and need on a small scale. While we come regularly in worship to have our feet washed, are we repenting for the collective failure of our race to further a world that the Creator found to be 'very good' (Gen. 1.31)? Are we even sufficiently aware of the failures in ourselves from which we need to repent?

Atonement

It has been clearly established that realisation of our failure and repentance only go some way in our journey of faith and that the grace of God's forgiveness is necessary for our salvation and peace. The forgiveness of Christ that is His prayer from the Cross is the entrée to an even greater grace, the grace of atonement, which must now be considered particularly.

On the road to Emmaus the two disciples returning home in their disillusionment following the Crucifixion, refer to Jesus merely as a 'prophet powerful in word and deed before God' (Lk. 24.19). He suffers the flogging and the nails, the taunts of the crowd and the soldiers, the fear and the betrayal of his followers, yet He knows that, as Son of God, he is the very essence of God himself. In his reflections on the Prodigal, Henri Nouwen sees Jesus as the Father becoming, in the person of the younger son, the prodigal son for our sake. Jesus, he writes, 'left the house of his heavenly Father, came to a foreign country, gave away all that he had, and returned through his cross to his Father's home'.[19] Though himself sinless, he is at one with his rebellious, half-penitent child. This is his atonement for the sins of the world, bearing the sufferings of the whole of humanity. Only God who sees the full extent of human sin can forgive sufficiently to cover our sin and failure.

According to D.M. Baillie, God in Christ's suffering and death is 'infinite Love confronted with human sin. And it is an *expiatory* sacrifice, because sin is a dreadfully real thing which love cannot tolerate or lightly pass over, and it is only out of the suffering of such inexorable love that true forgiveness, as distinct from an indulgent amnesty, could ever come.'[20] While, contrary to Baillie's assertion, some individuals manage to achieve feats of apparently superhuman forgiveness that cannot justifiably be relegated to the description 'indulgent amnesty', the atonement wrought by God in Christ is unique and beyond human means and understanding, in bearing the sins of humanity of all time in one act of grace that encompasses and absorbs our sin and our imperfect penitence, so long as it is grasped in faith, no matter how imperfectly.

But one further question is posed by Christ's unique act of expiation. Is this an act that demonstrates the supreme power of God, but has no ultimate effect on humanity because it is so supreme and renders humanity incapable of response? Jürgen Moltmann, in his stark portrayal of the significance of the sacrifice of Christ, demonstrates the way open for our response when he describes the challenge to us. Christ's sacrifice is 'the unconditioned and therefore boundless love which proceeds from the grief of the Father and the dying of the Son and reaches forsaken men in order to create in them the possibility and the force of new life'.[21] Christ's dying is not an isolated event in a wilderness of human failure and sin, but it is a transforming act that infuses the human spirit with the power to forgive, even when repentance is limited by our humanity. Those who are 'forsaken' because of their denial of Christ and their failure in love and service, are enabled to respond to the love of Christ, to be received again and to live renewed lives in the power of the resurrection. While repentance may be subject to our human limitations, His grace meets our imperfect response and creates new life, issuing in responses that may well be beyond what we believed to be our capability.

Repentance and Fruit

When Jesus is addressing the crowd at one point, he is recorded in two gospels as warning them of judgement to come when he says: 'You brood of vipers! Who warned you to flee from the coming wrath? Produce fruit in keeping with repentance' (Mt. 3.7-8 and Lk. 3.7-8). Our repentance has to be matched with a response to the inward call to bear fruit. We see this clearly in the case of Jonah who when he hears the voice within telling him to go to Nineveh, at first runs away to Tarshish, but then when called once again, obeys and indeed goes to Nineveh. We are driven back to the two brothers in their differing responses to their father's request, mentioned at the beginning of our study. Then there is Simon Peter whose threefold denial of Christ is cancelled out by the threefold command of the Saviour to love and serve, sealed by Christ's further injunction to him: 'Follow me' (Jn 21.15-19), the renewal of his discipleship. Peter of course matches his repentance with his actions in his new dedicated life. And Luke, describing Paul's confession to Agrippa says: 'So, then, King Agrippa, I was not disobedient to the vision from heaven [...] I preached that they should return to God and prove their repentance by their deeds' (Acts 26.19).

One parable illustrates that fruit and good actions do not necessarily occur at once. In the parable of the fig-tree that a man plants in his vineyard, no fruit is visible. When the man wants to cut it down after three years of fruitless waiting, the steward pleads for the tree to be given another chance, after which it would be cut down (Lk. 13.6-9). What strikes me in this is the second chance offered to the unfruitful fig-tree, perhaps an antidote of grace in contrast to the severe judgement meted out to it in Matthew's and Mark's accounts of the cursing of the fig-tree. I am sure that Luke's fig-tree would have been given even a further chance to prove itself.

The final note, in fact, is one of forgiveness and grace. One is left with the awareness that God loves everything He has made and it is in

His nature to offer redemptive grace to His creation. The experience of regeneration is a total experience of self-knowledge, repentance, forgiveness and call to action. G.W.H. Lampe writes about Zacchaeus that he was 'not called upon to make restitution before Christ entered his home; he repented and made amends because Christ had already accepted him as a sinner' (Lk. 19.5-6).[22] Self-knowledge and repentance are manifest in varying ways, not always directly visible, sometimes subsumed in one of the other elements, and also, as Lampe suggests, subsumed in forgiveness and acceptance. All individuals coming to God have their own experience of transformation, often incomprehensible to themselves.

From the dramatic, transforming revelation on the Damascus road Paul moves on to a new mission with constant repentance in the light of his self-knowledge and of God's endless grace. Unless the grace and forgiveness issue in response, even simply the response of 'touching the edge of His cloak', the forgiveness has been only half grasped and we remain in a limbo of semi-commitment. However, from the scene of transformation, they and we constantly return to the foot of the Cross where salvation is wrought and where our resurrection to new life begins. Even Michael Henchard, aware that he is in 'Somebody's hand', is surely received into the grace and loving hands of God whom he has sensed as a presence in his life.[23]

In the final analysis, the parable of the Lost Son and the Forgiving Father is perhaps the greatest of all parables for what it says about our flawed humanity and God's loving grace. The Prodigal after all has nothing to offer on his return to the Father. His only response and action is to return to the Father who is the one who lavishes forgiveness and grace on him. God is a God of grace and new life and we live not by certainty, but by faith that, however weak our experience and our commitment may be, we are accepted and empowered by the One whose power surpasses our own.

This article was first published in *The European Journal of Theology*, February 2014.

Endnotes

1   Wolfgang Pannenberg, *Jesus – God and Man*, translated by L.L. Wilkins and D.A. Priebe (London: SCM Press, 1968), 250.

2   Henri J. M. Nouwen, *The Return of the Prodigal Son* (London: Darton, Longman & Todd, 1994), 52.

3   Nouwen, *Prodigal*, 48

4   Nouwen, *Prodigal*, 51.

5   D. Jasper and A. Smith, *Between Truth and Fiction* (London: SCM Press, 2010), 16.

6   Sophocles, *King Oedipus*, from *The Theban Plays*, translated by E. F. Watling, (London: Penguin, 1947), 48.

7   Sophocles, *Antigone*, from *The Theban Plays* (London: Penguin 1947), 160.

8   Henri Blocher, *In the Beginning: The Opening Chapters of Genesis* (Nottingham: Inter-Varsity Press 1984), 204.

9   Gerhard von Rad, *Genesis*, translated by J.H. Marks (London: SCM Press 1972), 107.

10 Thomas Hardy, *The Mayor of Casterbridge* (London: Penguin 1997), 301.

11 Hardy, *Casterbridge*, 320.

12 Hardy, *Casterbridge*, 295.

13 Hardy, *Casterbridge*, 320.

14 John O'Donohue, *Eternal Echoes* (London: Bantam Books, 1998), 158.

15 Pannenberg, *Jesus*, 254.

16 My italics.

17 Tom Wright, *Justification* (London: SPCK, 2009), 157, author's italics.

18 The book by Margaret Heffernan, with the title *Wilful Blindness* (London: Simon & Schuster, 2011) explores this problem.

19 Nouwen, *Prodigal*, 55.

20 D.M. Baillie, *God was in Christ* (London: Faber & Faber, 1948), 198. Author's italics.

21 Jürgen Moltmann, *The Crucified God* (London: SCM Press, 1974), 253.

22 G.W.H. Lampe, 'The Atonement: Law and Love' in *Soundings*, ed. by A. Vidler (Cambridge University Press, 1962), 190.

23 See note 9.

Carrying the Fire
Is God present in the post-apocalyptic world of Cormac McCarthy's novel *The Road*?[1]

A man and his young son are struggling across the incinerated landscape of the United States, heading southwards to reach the coast. The child's mother is no longer with them: she took her own life shortly after the boy was born, unable to face the possibility of being raped and eaten by cannibals in this bleak situation where only a few people are alive and everyone is desperately looking for food. The story, in Cormac McCarthy's novel written in 2006 which won the Pulitzer Prize for 2007, among other things, acts as a warning of the potentially dire consequences of a nuclear holocaust or of drastic climate change.

McCarthy speaks of 'the intestate earth' (138), a planet that has no heirs and no future. We do not learn how the world became incinerated and barren, suggesting the inevitability of the destruction, a situation that would happen anyway regardless of possible causes. After all, we have tsunamis, earthquakes, and the threat of severe global warming. According to scientific calculation, it is claimed that the world's worst volcanic eruption occurred on Mount Toba 74,000 years ago.[2] The world has clearly been prepared for incineration in some form! I am reminded of the conclusion of Friedrich Dürrenmatt's black comedy *The Physicists* where 'round a small, yellow, nameless star there circles, pointlessly, everlastingly, the radioactive earth' after nuclear power and the fate of the world have fallen into the hands of an insane psychiatric doctor.[3] Is the cataclysm depicted in this novel the result of a nuclear holocaust, or the logical, disastrous consequence of climate change? Or is it the logical consequence of the presence of the fire deep down at the centre of the earth, fire that comes to the surface in the molten lava of a volcanic eruption, such as we saw in the BBC television series *The Power of the Planet* in which the presenter descends into the crater of a volcano in Ethiopia and almost touches the fiery lava as it lurks and bubbles threateningly? Or is it a divine visitation, perhaps punitive, in which God purges us of our achievements and we start afresh, as Teilhard de Chardin writes:

> Man can never reach the blazing centre of the universe simply by living more and more for himself, nor even by spending his life in the service of some earthly cause however great. The world can never be definitely united with you, Lord, save by a sort of reversal, a turning about […] which must involve the temporary collapse not merely of all individual achievements, but even of everything that looks like an advancement for humanity.[4]

Our imagination is simply left with the desperate post-apocalyptic picture, which seems to offer no hope to the few survivors. Dürrenmatt's 'yellow star', the sun, round which his earth spins, is contrasted with McCarthy's equally poignant image where after perhaps incinerating the planet with global warming or helpless to prevent destruction by other means 'the banished sun circles the earth like a grieving mother with a lamp' (32).[5] The man carries a revolver containing two bullets which he even tries to teach the boy to use, should their situation become irreparable.

So does the novel offer a picture that is in any way different from what McCarthy demonstrates in previous works? Is there any way in which God can be perceived as present in this grim scene? Critics see very little to hope for in this bleak world. If we look back to his great novel *Blood Meridian*, the ex-priest pronounces his verdict: 'Certainly the wise high God in his dismay at the proliferation of lunacy on this earth must have wetted a thumb and leaned down out of the abyss and pinched it hissing into oblivion.'[6] It is a topsy-turvy world in which the abyss is above us or we are so far down even below the bottom of the abyss and God extinguishes us. But at least God is mentioned and acts, whereas in the final orgiastic, Dionysian dance of depravity in the novel the world has finally lost all contact with the divine.[7] However, in *No Country for Old Men*, the novel McCarthy wrote before *The Road*, there is some hope of God's presence following the brutal events of the greater part of the novel. When Sheriff Bell, anxious to make amends for failures earlier in his life, meets his uncle Ellis, he tells him: 'I always thought when I got older that God would sort of come into my life in some way. He didn't.'[8] But he continues to wonder:

> Do you think God knows what's happenin'?
> I expect he does.
> You think he can stop it?
> No. I don't.[9]

But in his desire to be reconciled to his father, Bell has a dream in which he sees his father: 'And in the dream I knew that he was goin' on ahead and that he was fixin' to make a fire out there in all that dark and all that cold and I knew that whenever I got there he would be there.' Then he almost dashes the hope when he wakes up.[10] Yet the thought is present, to be taken up where he leaves off, in *The Road*.

So despite the bleak picture which the author describes in unbelievably beautiful prose, *The Road* begins with more hope of the presence of God than the tale generally allows for. In one of his rare interviews, McCarthy is said to have claimed that the book is 'about goodness'.[11] And the distinguished film critic, Philip French, in his review of the film version of the novel released in early January 2010, writes of the novel's 'harrowing, but ultimately life-enhancing qualities'.[12] But when one critic expresses the thoughts of very many in his comment that 'in McCarthy's novel there is no hope [...] And yet the father and son go on, seeking to find meaning and purpose',[13] the outlook for discovering the presence of God beyond human endeavour is on balance not very promising. Thus, the signs pointing to God's presence and involvement in this apparently hopeless situation must now be considered in detail to offset the grim scene before us.

While the author paints a bleak picture, the name of God and signs of God's influence are never far from his pen. Very early in the novel the father says of his son: 'If he is not the word of God, God never spoke' (3). The boy embodies for the father all the hope he might have in God, all the evidence he has of God's reality. At a particularly difficult moment, he tells his son: 'My job is to take care of you. I was appointed to do that by God' (80). But the boy is also leading the father, directing his moral sense, while being protected physically by him. In the opening paragraph the father relates that in a dream 'from which he's awakened he had wandered in a cave where the child led him by the hand' (1). In this bleakest of opening two pages, the word 'light' occurs four times to at least counteract the force of what he says in the third line of his story: 'Nights dark beyond darkness and the days more gray each one than what had gone before' (1). While the father's love is solely for his son, the 'word of God' given into his keeping, and he sees his role as that of protecting the boy against all comers, his protective urge is throughout countered by the boy's strong moral concern for those they encounter and are unable to help, to such an extent that the child pesters his father to help fellow sufferers long after the event has ceased to have significance. Any respite and sustenance they find are short-lived. The father's developing illness marks this decline into apparent hopelessness. However, the boy gradually grows accustomed to the situation and less dependent on his father, whose hacking cough and growing physical weakness signal that the child will eventually have to fend for himself, as long as this is possible in the conditions.

It seems that a balance is being maintained between total despair and the advent of some hope that the boy will be able to cope, at least in the short term. While their hopeless situation is symbolised by the empty tin that is left between the father's feet once they have reached the coast and found tins of peaches to eat (254), the fact that the father entrusts his revolver to the boy is a sign of trust that extinction is not absolutely guaranteed (305). But the father's act of firing off the flare pistol in the hope that somebody, perhaps God (in the boy's mind) might see them, signals another descent into futility (258).

But while an old man whom they encounter mocks the suggestion of the presence of God in a corrupt version of terms familiar to Moslems when he says: 'There is no god, and we are his prophets' (180-181), a firm seed of hope is planted quite early in the story and recurs four more times in the text when the father reiterates the son's assertion that they are 'carrying the fire', words that the father has obviously repeated previously.[13] As mentioned above, the germ of this idea has already been present at the end of McCarthy's previous novel. The view of many readers is that this signals a tribute to the power of human effort against insuperable odds.

However, while sceptics rule out divine involvement, two converging views of the nature of literary creation and our interpretation of what we read can help us to a different conclusion where God becomes important to our quest. Marcel Proust writes: 'We feel that our wisdom begins where the author's finishes, and we would like him to give us answers, when all he can do is to give us wishes.' A few lines later he continues: 'The limit of their wisdom only appears to us to be the beginning of ours, so that at the moment when they have told us everything they could tell us, they have aroused in us the feeling that they have not yet told us anything.'[14] What a novelist writes is a stimulus to us to ask questions and to discover our own answers within ourselves. And in *The Art of the Novel*, Milan Kundera writes: 'A poet who serves any truth other than the truth to be *discovered* [...] is a false poet.'[15] It is a reasonable proposition that, given a substantial body of supporting evidence, a valid response can be evoked in the reader that is true for us that is not necessarily in the mind or intentions of the writer and certainly not of other readers. I believe that the evidence, not only for God's initial commission to the father to protect his son, but also for a belief in the presence of God even in the depths of this poignant tale can be detected in this novel as the story unfolds and reaches its climax, despite the dire prognosis present in much of the text and in the minds of many readers. The evidence for this must now be considered.

Mention has already been made of the frequent naming of God in the course of the story, even if the allusions are sceptical or despairing in their tone and implications. But also the use of the word 'fire' carries both negative and positive implications – the fire of destruction visited upon this world and yet also the 'fire in the earth' of Teilhard de Chardin when, in contrast to the fire of destruction, he says: 'If the Fire has come down into the heart of the world, it is [...] to lay hold on me and to absorb me.'[16] It is the fire of purging and re-creation. Before he dies, the father expresses his confidence that his son will continue to carry the fire. When the child says that he doesn't know where the fire is, father utters words that are crucial to our understanding of the novel. 'It's inside you. It was always there. I can see it' (298), This follows the father's expression of hope that his son will be able to continue the fight, as he watches his son while they are sitting by the fire. 'He wanted to be able to see. Look around you, he said. There is no prophet in the earth's long chronicle who's not honoured here today. Whatever form you spoke of you were right' (297). In his own mind he is directly refuting the nihilistic assertion of the old man previously mentioned who declares that 'There is no God and we are his prophets'. In the Book of Jeremiah, the prophet announces the coming of the New Covenant that the Lord will make with Israel:

> I will put my law in their minds and write it on their
> hearts. I will be their God and they will be my people.
> No longer will a man teach his neighbour, or a man his
> brother, saying: "Know the Lord", because they will all
> know me, from the greatest of them to the least (Jer.
> 31.33-34).

And when, as recorded in Luke's Gospel, the Pharisees ask Jesus when the kingdom of God will come, he answers: 'The kingdom of God does not come with your careful observation, nor will people say, "Here it is" or "There it is", because the kingdom of God is within you' (Lk. 17.20-21).

The father has seen that, just as our Lord is recorded as stating that 'where your treasure is there will your heart be also' his son's strong moral convictions and love of fellow sufferers have for a long time been evidence of a divine spirit written like an instinctive, natural law on his son's nature carrying him forward. After the father's death when the boy is found by a stranger and his family, he asks the stranger rather as if he is naively repeating what he has heard time and again from his father: 'Are you carrying the fire?' (303). Though the stranger, unfamiliar with the secret held by the father and his son, is at first unable to understand the drift of the boy's question, he answers in the affirmative, and the boy is also at once reassured on hearing that he has a family and that there is another boy present. There is also a girl in the family, suggesting hope for the future of the race. These people have somehow been able to stay together and are surviving for now at least. The boy who has throughout been asking his father if the people they meet are 'the good guys' is able to take comfort in the fact that these people are indeed good and he can trust them.[17] The boy trusts the stranger to cover his father's body with a blanket. The stranger trusts the boy to keep the revolver. The basis is there for the creation of a new family and for the boy's adoption into it.

In the final two pages of the novel, the new mother assumes importance. When the boy mourns his dead father and promises to talk to him every day, the mother welcomes and embraces him. Sometimes she talks to him about God, but when he tries to pray he finds that the best thing is to talk to his father. His new mother approves, saying that 'the breath of God was his breath yet though it pass from man to man through all of time' (306). Human beings have been created by God to hand down the flame from generation to generation. At this point, the question whether any of them would survive long enough to carry any fire forward is almost transformed into the hope of new relationships, new faith and purpose. Through the sheer beauty and simplicity of the language the reader is almost made to suspend all gloom and disbelief and live in hopes that the bleak world of the author's creation up to this point is not the end of all things.

The last paragraph of the novel is enigmatic, confirmed by the final word 'mystery'. There is a picture of trout morphing into shapes like worms resembling the beginnings of maps of the world: 'Maps and mazes. Of a thing which could not be put back. Not be made right again. In the deep glens where they live all things were older than man and they hummed of mystery' (307). Man is the newest of creatures. He is the latest created being. What has been done to the world cannot be undone. The picture again reverts partly to one in which, in the words of *Blood Meridian* already quoted, man is 'pinched […] hissing into extinction'. Yet goodness has emerged from the ruins and new relationships of goodness, faith and service have been created. An objective look at the state of the post-apocalyptic world depicted in the novel might tell us that these new hopes are ultimately to be dashed. But within the terms of the novel and of our experience of immersion in its beauty God has been seen throughout the work, and especially in its conclusion. But one could be forgiven for looking back at the brief exchange between Bell and Uncle Ellis in the previous novel in which God is said to know what is happening, but is unable to prevent it. On that basis, a sceptic might well say that if God is powerless, any love He might have for the incinerated world is meaningless.

But in one final glimpse of my truth discovered in this novel, following Proust's advice, I am reminded of the words from Paul's letter to the Corinthians: 'God chose the weak things of the world to shame the strong. He chose the lowly things of the world, and the despised things – and the things that are not – to nullify the things that are' (1 Cor. 1.27-28). With the eye of faith, one can see the end of this world as the beginning of the new. One can see God creating a world from the ruins of what no longer exists. Just as the German nation saw 1945 as 'zero hour' from which everything must rise from the ruins, I believe that our author sees that mankind, though it cannot remake what is destroyed, can carry the fire forward and that, just as the book closes in mystery, all things are possible and that the name of God has not been named in vain throughout the course of this work. What the future holds, none can ever know. But the final paragraph of our novel holds also the suggestion that a new world is beginning. McCarthy speaks of 'vermiculate patterns that were maps of the world in its *becoming*'.[18] The proximity of death and physical extinction does not exclude the reality of faith here and now. 'The light shines in the darkness and the darkness has not overcome it' (Jn 1.5). In this novel we have in the here and now a priceless tenderness in the hearts of human beings and hope in new relationships in a writer who has a glimmer of hope in humankind and has succeeded in recreating a new work of beauty from the ruins of the old. Thus, just as 'against all hope, Abraham in hope believed' (Rom. 4.18) that his race had a future, we are lured into a belief that a new world of people indwelt by the divine spirit might after all just be possible and if brief, once seen, cannot be extinguished in our consciousness.

This article was first published in *The Epworth Review,* January 2011.

Endnotes

1   Cormac McCarthy, *The Road* (London: Picador, 2007). Henceforth, as this is the main text of this study, textual references to the novel will be in brackets in the text.

2   See Simon Winchester, *Krakatoa* (London: Penguin, 2004), 309.

3   Friedrich Dürrenmatt, *The Physicists,* translated by James Kirkup (London: Samuel French, 1963), 53.

4   Teilhard de Chardin, *Hymn of the Universe* (London: Collins Fontana, 1970), 30.

5   Cormac McCarthy, *Blood Meridian* (London: Picador, 1990), 244.

6   McCarthy, *Blood Meridian,* 331-335.

7   Cormac McCarthy, *No Country for Old Men* (London: Picador, 2005), 267.

8   McCarthy, *No Country,* 269.

9   McCarthy, *No Country,* 309.

10 Article in *The Observer*, 20.12.2009, 43.

11 Article in *The Observer* review section, 03.01.10, 13.

12 J. Cowley, *The New Statesman,* 26 November 2007, 51.

13 McCarthy, *The Road,* 87. Also 136, 231, 298, 303.

14 Marcel Proust, *On Reading* ('Sur la lecture', France, Actes Sud, 1998), 32, my translation.

15 Milan Kundera, *The Art of the Novel,* translated by L. Asher (London: Faber & Faber, 1988), 117.

16 de Chardin, *Hymn,* 28.

17 The first of the eleven references to this occurs on p. 81.

18 Author's italics.

A Person Can Change
Grace, forgiveness and sonship in Marilynne Robinson's novel *Gilead*

Two-thirds of the way through Marilynne Robinson's 2005 Pulitzer Prize-winning novel *Gilead*, Jack Boughton asks the Congregationalist minister John Ames the awkward question: 'Do you think some people are intentionally and irretrievably consigned to perdition?'. John Ames, unable to answer the question and aware of the tension existing between him and Jack caused by the latter's insensitive practical jokes on him as a teenager and by his later irresponsible lifestyle, prevaricates, until his wife, Lila, eventually, after some thought, answers the question with the simple words: 'A person can change'.[1]

The novel has reached a crossroads some time previously when Jack (christened John Ames), the son of the older John Ames' best friend, has returned to the small town of Gilead in Iowa where the older John Ames has been a pastor for all his working life and his return has evoked problems that have lain dormant in Ames' consciousness for a long time. Jack's return sets in motion a host of worries and conscience pangs that lead eventually to an act of forgiveness and a form of adoption that lie at the heart of Robinson's wonderfully spiritual novel, her second, coming twenty-three years after her first, *Housekeeping*.[2]

Like *Housekeeping*, *Gilead* is built round the fortunes of families that are closely interlinked. Whereas the earlier novel covers three generations, *Gilead* covers four, all four generations in a family of pastors in which the tradition of service as ministers seems to perpetuate itself almost automatically. John Ames, the first person narrator of the novel, is approaching the age of seventy-seven. He is seriously ill with angina and aware that death is near. He is writing an extended testimony to his young son, aged seven, born of his second wife, Lila, who is more than thirty years younger than himself. John Ames had married young, but his first wife, Louisa, had died in childbirth and their daughter had died very shortly after, leaving John Ames a lonely, withdrawn pastor for forty years until he meets his second wife and marries at the age of sixty-seven. He has committed almost all his spiritual thoughts to a massive collection of sermons that he has kept and from time to time reactivates, and he continues in this vein with his present written testimony to his son who remains nameless and is destined one day to read his father's reminiscences, advice and exhortations.

This testimony is a mixture of reminiscences about the fortunes of the previous three generations of John Ames' family, guidance for his son and mental struggles over his attitude to Jack Boughton. The earlier part of the novel dwells largely on the relationships within the previous generations of the family, in particular the different attitudes of his father and grandfather to their calling. When at one point quite late in the novel John Ames muses that 'we all [...] live in the ruins of the lives of other generations' (225), he is recalling the acute differences between his grandfather, his father and himself and hoping that his own son will find a good way in life that will bring him fulfilment and an avoidance of the errors of previous generations.

The essential difference between father and grandfather is that grandfather sees himself as committed fully to a vision that causes him as a warrior in God's army to regard his son, John Ames' father, as pietistic and quietist, lacking a true vision to reach out to those in need. Following a sermon that the father preaches, the rift between them seems to have become impossible to bridge and grandfather leaves home in anger, which John's father regrets for the rest of his life and for which he and John later try to make amends by seeking out his grave, while still unable to accept the tenor of grandfather's ministry and religious views.

Yet while grandfather takes his vision to extremes and leaves home causing bad feeling and unhappiness, father too, in an extreme expression of his peace-loving spirit, disappoints his son John by leaving his pastoral role late in his ministry and going over to the Quakers, leaving grandfather to look after his church and people. It seems that men of conviction are prone to actions of principle that can cause dissension and unhappiness. These are to some extent the ruins of preceding generations from which new generations arise and from which John Ames is hoping to rescue his young son. As an antidote to the dominance of father over son that he has experienced, he not only remembers grandfather's care of father's parishioners, but at one point considers the Fifth Commandment 'Honour your father and mother' and turns it round, saying that the parent should honour the child (152-155). He describes his young son as 'God's grace to me, a miracle' (60). The way is being paved for a set of changed attitudes in the second half of the novel.

While Lila's words 'a person can change' can be construed in one sense negatively as a sad reflection of the disappointment that we can feel about the changed attitudes of previous generations in our families, the early deaths of John Ames' first wife and his daughter open the way eventually for a new direction in the novel and a new kind of father-son relationship. When Louisa dies, John Ames is away from home and his daughter is baptised by his long-standing friend, Boughton, a Presbyterian minister. John Ames just has time to hold her in his arms before she dies. During the rest of his ministry he is withdrawn, a peaceable man very much in the spirit of his father, but different from father and grandfather in that he remains loyal to his place of calling. But he is not able to communicate easily, putting his thoughts more clearly into his mountain of sermons and preferring to sit quietly in his church rather than visiting church members who may regard him as an intrusion. It almost looks as if his ministry is to die with him in a buried legacy of sermons, until he meets his second wife in a series of happy incidents that form one of the most endearing episodes in the novel. Lila is totally new to the religious tradition. She is unlearned, and when she arrives is first baptised. She brings a totally fresh attitude into his ministry and attitudes and becomes a conduit for a new attitude to the one man who has been, as he says, a thorn in his heart for so long (142), Jack Boughton, the maverick son of his old friend Pastor Boughton.

Through hints of John Ames' critical attitude to Jack, we gradually become aware of John Ames' prejudice and resentment, until a full account is given of Jack's betrayal of a woman whom he had made pregnant in a youthful indiscretion and his refusal to accept the care of their daughter. John Ames cannot forgive or forget the many pranks that Jack, during his childhood, plays on him, principally that he removes a little photograph of his daughter Louisa, that he admittedly returns to him later. The problem is increased by the fact that his friend Boughton had christened his son John Ames in his desire to give John a new son to replace his lost daughter and had called his friend 'the father of his soul', that is his son's (140). It is as if John Ames senior has had to accept as his adopted child one who becomes a perpetual reminder of his resentment towards him. And when Jack has a baby daughter whom he rejects John Ames tries hard not to resent the fact that he himself has lost a daughter whom he would have loved and cherished dearly.

When Jack comes back into John Ames' purview after being away for so long, he calls him 'Papa' (104) and addresses John's young son as 'little brother' (108). The stage is being set for John Ames to face the fact of his resentment and the *fait accompli* created by

Boughton when he baptised his son with John Ames' name. Through his recollection of this, John Ames is being nudged towards an act of forgiveness and acceptance of his role as Jack's spiritual father before both the old men die. This acceptance of the new relationship before John Ames dies frees his conscience from the nagging awareness of his previous refusal to forgive Jack.

Jack, now returned, starts this process on his side with his simple words to John Ames 'I'm very sorry' (191), which, however, fail to clear the air and remove the embarrassment that both feel in each other's presence. It is Lila who, with her words 'a person can change', sows a seed in her husband's heart. John Ames, the hesitant communicator who has to put everything in writing, struggles to express what he is becoming increasingly aware of, that forgiveness must come and he must initiate it.

This is clear to him earlier when he asks himself: 'What is the Lord asking of me in this moment, in this situation?'. While one's impulse tells one to answer antagonism in kind, the matter looks entirely different when you tell yourself:

> This is an emissary sent from the Lord, and some
> benefit is intended for me, first of all to demonstrate
> my faithfulness, the chance to show that I do in some
> small degree participate in the grace that saved me, you
> are free to act otherwise than as circumstances would
> seem to dictate. You are free to act by your own lights.
> You are freed at the same time of the impulse to hate
> or resent that person (141).

In her earlier collection of essays *The Death of Adam*, Marilynne Robinson demonstrates the absolute importance of grace in her essay on Dietrich Bonhoeffer, when she highlights the latter's rejection of what he calls 'cheap grace' in favour of 'costly grace' and reiterates Bonhoeffer's contention that 'faith only becomes faith in the act of obedience'.[3] Saint Paul also writes of 'the obedience that comes from faith' (Rom. 1.5). The act of grace is not simply a free gift to use regardless of our wishes or choice in the matter. Certainly, forgiveness of the other person demonstrates our faithfulness, but it is also an act of obedience to God's call to create reconciliation. Obedience has to be planted within us. Ultimately, John Ames explains this by the theological term 'prevenient grace that precedes grace itself and allows us to accept it'. After all, grace must be accepted and find a place in our hearts. It does not simply come like a thunderbolt from the blue. Then he adds immediately: 'I think there must also be a prevenient courage that allows us to be brave – that is, to acknowledge that there is more beauty than our eyes can bear and to do nothing to honour them is to do great harm' (280-281). This is not a note of grudging forgiveness, or of forgiveness to prove our own spirituality, but a positive appreciation of the beauty of the other person, the object of God's grace and of our forgiveness. But it is clear that this prevenient grace is a gift without which we would not be in the frame of mind to forgive and love.

He had found a sermon written in 1947 on the subject of forgiveness, in which he maintains that the Prodigal Son is restored to his place in his father's house, 'though he neither asks to be restored as son nor even repents of the grief he has caused his father'. This paves the way for the realisation that John Ames must be willing to forgive, that 'grace is the great gift. So to be forgiven is only half the gift. The other half is that *we* also can forgive, restore and liberate, and therefore we can feel the will of God enacted through us, which is the great restoration of ourselves to ourselves' (183-4). The author, as we do, knows that such forgiveness comes after a struggle, one aspect of which is that John Ames, somewhat alarmed, sees the growing understanding between Jack and his wife, Lila, the closeness of their ages, the fact that Lila's unorthodox attitudes match Jack's rebelliousness and that, when he dies, they, with his young son, could form a new family group. So John Ames, while wanting to forgive, is still unable to overcome his fears and resentment. His lengthy dwelling on the story of Hagar and Ishmael (Gen. 21) and the fact that Abraham sends them off into the wilderness, together with the similar experience of Abraham sent by the Lord into the wilderness with Isaac to test Abraham (Gen. 22) highlights his awareness of the difficulty of launching his young family out into an uncertain future, possibly with Jack Boughton. In our consideration of grace, it is important to note that 'the emissary sent from the Lord' appears to indicate a direct act of God's spirit coming into John Ames' life and transforming his attitude, albeit with some difficulty, but not specifically mediated by the life and work of our Lord Jesus Christ and his forgiveness of his enemies from the Cross. It is possible that the author assumes that 'the Lord' is a term covering both the Father and the Son. It is also possible that she wishes to focus our attention on the struggle between the natural impulses of John Ames and the constraining influence of an inward spiritual power which invades his consciousness and transforms his heart, without emphasising the strengthening presence of a mediating, redeeming Christ who might be seen as a *deus ex machina*.

From the moment when Lila says 'a person can change' and brings her breath of fresh air into the closed room of resentment harboured over many years, the novel is concerned with increasing intensity with the struggle in John Ames to overcome his resentment and to find common ground with Jack. Suddenly, in a spiritual impulse which appears rather like a *deus ex machina*, he declares in his testimony to his young son: 'John Ames Boughton is my son. If there is any truth at all in anything I believe, that is true also. By "my son" I mean another self, a more cherished self' (215). He realises that the initiative to forgive and accept is the Lord's. 'If the Lord chooses to make nothing of our transgressions, then they are nothing' (216). He now knows that his own feelings in the matter are less important than the love that the Lord has for this man whom he has resented for so long. Despite his initial fear that Jack could take over his family and influence his young son, he is now increasingly able to see Jack through God's eyes. And it is clear also that Jack is seeking reconciliation. But there are many abortive attempts to bring this about, due to the legacy of previous resentments and embarrassment on both sides, before reconciliation is achieved.

A very important reason for John Ames' changed attitude and for his finding it easier to forgive, is that Jack has married and fathered a child, a boy, for whom after his earlier transgression he has accepted responsibility. In John's eyes this new relationship helps to make amends for the betrayals of the past. In the absence of any belief in God's mercy Jack has himself taken the initiative in self-redemption and wants acceptance from the man whom he has wronged. This is granted with an embrace, the blessing from Num. 6.24-26 and his own words, 'Lord, bless John Ames Boughton, this beloved son and brother and husband and father' (276), as Jack leaves home again shortly before his father's death. While Jack's sister feels that Jack has again betrayed his loved ones, John Ames can now understand that Jack has his secret, but justifiable reasons for his action, which he, John Ames, will not judge harshly. Not only has John lost his resentment, he is now able to accept Jack's word without knowledge or justification. So relieved and elated is John Ames that he would have 'gone through seminary and ordination and all the years intervening for that one moment' (276).

While it may appear that Jack's offences towards John Ames have been relatively minor, they were as much as the latter can bear at the time, given his years of loneliness and leisure for 'nursing a grudge' (134). Many crises in the family's history remain unresolved. The arrival of his new wife from an entirely non-religious background brings new life, fresh understanding and grace, so that the present and the future can redeem the past, and the fear of launching his young son and wife into an uncertain future can be allayed.

The theme of sonship and adoption has been signposted from the moment when Jack ironically calls John Ames 'Papa'. We are strongly reminded of Saint Paul's words: 'For you did not receive a spirit that makes you a slave again to fear, but you received the spirit of sonship. And by him we cry, "*Abba,* Father". The Spirit himself testifies that we are God's children. Now if we are children, then we are heirs' (Rom. 8.15-16). John's young son is an heir of the grace that has flowed through his father's testimony, as are we who have had the privilege through this wonderful novel of sharing in this act of our Lord's grace wrought in the lives and fortunes of these families. Even if the great redeeming events of our Lord's life and death are not specified in this novel, the power of the Spirit given to us can change us so that we are freed from the chains of the past and are pleased to obey his call to forgive.

This article was first published in *The Evangelical Quarterly*, January 2008.

Endnotes

1   Marilynne Robinson, *Gilead* (London: Virago, 2005), 174. Henceforth, as this is the main text for study, references to the text will be given in brackets in the article. Since writing this novel, Robinson has written two companion texts, *Home* (Virago, 2009) with events seen through the eyes of Jack Boughton, and *Lila* (Farrar, Straus & Giroux, 2014) with events seen through the eyes of Lila herself

2   Marilynne Robinson, *Housekeeping* (London: Faber & Faber, 1983).

3   Marilynne Robinson, *The Death of Adam* (New York; Mariner Books, 1998), 111, and Dietrich Bonhoeffer, *The Cost of Discipleship* (London; SCM Press, 1959), 54.

Michael Henchard's Will
Self-love and its absence in the light of Thomas Hardy's novel *The Mayor of Casterbridge*

Michael Henchard, the Mayor of Casterbridge in Hardy's novel, is the man who in a drunken bout sells his wife and baby daughter at a fair for five guineas. That comes at the end of the first chapter. He spends the rest of the novel regretting his action and fighting off the arrows that destiny fires at him despite himself. The following day, he goes to a church and vows to abstain from all alcohol. And at the end of the story, to complete the framework of this sad tale, he leaves a piece of paper on which he writes his will which is discovered by his daughter and her husband on his death-bed. He writes as follows:

> That Elizabeth-Jane Farfrae be not told of my death, or
> made to grieve on account of me.
> - that I be not bury'd in consecrated ground.
> - that no sexton be asked to toll the bell.
> - that nobody is wished to see my dead body.
> - that no murners walk behind me at my funeral.
> - that no flours be planted on my grave.
> - that no man remember me.
> To this I put my name.[1]

During his life, after losing his wife and daughter, he had settled in Casterbridge and in less than twenty years had risen to become its mayor. He has built up a flourishing business as a grain merchant. But from the moment when his wife, widowed from her sailor husband, returns with her daughter and finds Henchard in Casterbridge, his fortunes decline. By the end of the story, such is his state of mind and body that he has lost all self-esteem, is filled with self-loathing and wishes simply to fade into oblivion. While the story is clearly an extreme case and Hardy's view, seen through the fates of his protagonists in his novels, is that his leading characters are dogged by an almost inscrutable destiny that shows them little mercy, many Christians too have the same lack of self-love, whether for reasons of mistaken theology or through an exaggerated awareness of personal sin and unworthiness. I wish to consider this problem in light of Henchard's situation.

Henchard's tragic flaw is his impulsiveness, that leads him to act fatally in the first place, and then takes him into successive acts in a downward spiral as the story develops. Some of his impulses are potentially good, for instance his appointment of Donald Farfrae as his manager on the very day of his wife's reappearance. Not only is Farfrae a good manager, he is also a generous person who does not take advantage of Henchard's later impulsiveness in taking him into his confidence. Henchard's later rash act in making his appearance at the royal visit once he has been replaced as mayor by Farfrae following the demise of Henchard's business, the decline in his fortunes and his jealousy of Farfrae is the result of hurt pride and stubbornness. His last and fatal impulsive act is to send the sailor Newson away with the false information of the death of Newson's daughter, Elizabeth-Jane whom Henchard has brought up as his own and whom he does not want to lose. Newson, who had bought Henchard's wife and daughter before later faking his own death at sea to release his unhappy wife, has returned to look for his daughter whom he believes is still alive.

But once the train of events has been set in motion, Henchard is sometimes the victim of other people's actions. It seems that his destiny is unable to distinguish between his own guilt and that of others. The reappearance of his former lover, Lucetta, the actions of the local citizens in parodying her relationship with Henchard and the failure of Joshua Jopp to return Lucetta's love letters to her once Henchard has agreed to surrender them are events that would not have occurred but for Henchard's initial action and the situation in which it has placed him. Furthermore, his impulsiveness goes hand in hand with strong feelings of pride and jealousy which lead him into distrust and hatred of Farfrae, and into selfish acts of possessiveness, such as his failure to inform Elizabeth-Jane of her true origin and her father's return, seeking her.

The accumulation of such acts unfortunately creates situations in which Henchard's good impulses are misunderstood and ignored, with tragic consequences. When his wife Susan reappears and makes herself known to him, he immediately agrees to see her and sends her a sum of money corresponding to the five guineas paid for her and their child at auction, as if he is trying to wipe out the debt he owes her. Also when Lucetta who has married Farfrae falls ill because of the combination of her pregnancy and the citizens' ridicule of her previous relationship with Henchard, Henchard sets off to alert Farfrae who is away on business, but the latter distrusts and ignores his warning and is unable to return to his wife in time. And when Henchard realises that Newson whom he has sent away has returned, he leaves home to work and settle elsewhere, but then returns to make a surprise appearance at his daughter's wedding to Farfrae, Elizabeth-Jane who has always been a model of patience and forbearance, accuses him of betraying her best interests in not informing her of her true origins and in sending her father away, so that as a result Henchard leaves her for ever and dies, leaving his sad will on his death-bed.

Not only is Henchard's good impulse in relation to Lucetta and Farfrae ignored, but his own conviction of his own failure in his love for Elizabeth-Jane paralyses his response at the moment of his return to attend her wedding. His self-respect and self-confidence have collapsed, and he is unable to reply to her accusation. The gift he has brought her, a goldfinch in a cage, is simply left abandoned in the garden, a symbol of his failure and isolation in his self-loathing.

Self-loathing and an acute sense of guilt can destroy an awareness in human beings of the good acts that we perform, but which are submerged in the sea of self-doubt and despair that our other actions cause us. When, after his fatal misleading of Newson, he decides in bleak despair to take his own life by throwing himself into a pool by a weir, Henchard sees the effigy of himself floating in the water, after the citizens have discarded it following their parody of himself and Lucetta. When Elizabeth-Jane finds him and takes him home, saying she will not leave him, he realises that he has been saved, while Lucetta, the other effigy, has died. His comment: 'Who is such a reprobate as I! And yet it seems that even I be in Somebody's hand!'[2] indicates his awareness of the presence of a guiding supernatural power in his life, but he is also aware of the destructive thoughts that assail him in his attempt to prevent Elizabeth-Jane's marriage to Farfrae. 'Why should I still be subject to these visitations of the devil, when I try so hard to keep him away?'[3] His self-awareness kills off the momentary joy of finding himself saved and reprieved to continue with his adopted daughter. He knows of his weakness, but his natural instinctive impulses towards jealousy and possessiveness destroy the good that could restore his self-love.

Yet that is not the whole story. When Henchard finally goes away and Farfrae and Elizabeth-Jane find him sick and dying, it emerges that Abel Whittle, a local man who has worked for Henchard, has tended him in his last illness because of Henchard's caring love for Abel's mother. Seeing that Henchard looks ill as he is leaving Casterbridge for the last time, Abel follows him out on the road to the place where he dies, and looks after him in his final illness. Henchard's care for Abel Whittle's mother in giving her help while she is ill generates Abel's loving act in return. Henchard however cannot see this, blinded as he is to what goodness he has shown in his life. As he is dying, he asks Whittle: 'Can ye really be such a poor fond fool as to care for such a wretch as I!'[4]

He can only see himself as a 'wretch'. But he is thinking and feeling within a great tradition. Saint Paul, no less, writes of himself: 'What a wretched man I am!', having analysed his moral dilemma in terms that Henchard would later understand and see in himself: 'I have the desire to do what is good, but I cannot carry it out. For what I do is not the good I want to do; no, the evil I do not want to do – this I keep on doing. Now if I do what I do not want to do, it is no longer I that do it, but it is sin living in me that does it' (Rom. 7.18-25). Henchard, like Paul, sees a power within him that drives him towards actions he regrets. John Newton, the writer of the hymn *Amazing Grace*, sees himself in the same light as he writes:

> Amazing grace (how sweet the sound)
> That saved a wretch like me.[5]

And in the hymn of Charles Wesley, whose first line is 'Let earth and heaven agree', the tone of admission of the hard fact of one's wretchedness is expressed in the fifth verse of his hymn:

> Stung by the scorpion sin
> My poor expiring soul
> The healing sound drinks in.[6]

In all three cases, the spiritual misery is fully offset by the healing grace flooding in to overcome the acute sense of sin, a feeling that Henchard is unable to share, as his brief awareness of the presence of 'Somebody's hand' is soon swallowed up in a feeling that he is prevented by the devil from enjoying any respite from his turmoil. But he accepts his own responsibility and guilt. As he is leaving Casterbridge, he says to himself: 'I Cain – go alone, as I deserve – an outcast and a vagabond.'[7] He is not excusing himself, and has deserved what fate is inflicting on him. If he were purely the victim of events beyond his control, his self-loathing would not be so acute.

What emerges from the two examples from the hymn writers and Saint Paul is a form of dualism that sets grace against a conviction of inner wretchedness, with grace triumphant. However, for the human being at the centre of the conflict, the awareness of the severity of the struggle with sin and guilt very often becomes dominant to the extent that too many Christians labour under an extreme sense of sin, from which they find little relief. The opposite extreme might often be a cosy acceptance of easy grace with the awareness of the reasons for such grace smothered under a blanket of warm religiosity.

What is undeniable is that western Christian theology has been dominated by the Pauline conviction (expressed mainly in the letter to the Romans and reinforced in the Augustinian tradition within the Church) of the two poles of sin/death and redemption/life which has meant that many Christians have tended to swing between a strong sense of unforgiven sin and guilt and the redemption of forgiveness sought time and time again. For many this has come to mean that they have either accepted forgiveness automatically as an ecclesiastical good habit or that they have worried over the genuineness of their repentance and found it very difficult indeed to accept their fallibility as part and parcel of their humanity which God has created and which he loves. Thus, self-love and self-esteem have for too many Christians been elusive blessings. They have wondered how the Lord can accept and love them when they are so obviously frail and weak both in faith and in God's service of spreading his love.

The American scholar Lewis Smedes makes a distinction that could well help Christians struggling with a low sense of self-love. In one work he describes how in the past he did not feel guilt for specific sins, but 'a glob of unworthiness that I could not tie down to any concrete sins I was guilty of'.[8] In his chapter 'Singing "Amazing Grace" Without Feeling Like A Wretch', he writes:

> A grace that makes us feel worse for having it is an
> ungracious grace and therefore not really grace at all.

If grace heals our shame, it must be a grace that tells us we are worthy to have it. We need, I believe, to recognize that we are accepted not only in spite of our undeserving, but because of our worth.[9]

He continues almost immediately. 'If I deserve some good thing, it is because I *did* something to earn it. If I am *worthy*, it is because I *am* somebody of enormous value.'[10] So when the Apostle Paul wrote that 'Christ Jesus came into the world to save sinners – of whom I am the worst' (1 Tim. 1.15) he is not being falsely humble, but recalling that his past persecutions of Christians as well as his present acts mean that he has not deserved his salvation. When the present Archbishop of York in a different context writes in a Sunday newspaper 'I count myself most unworthy of all to approach the altar of God', he may well be doing himself a disservice and, in Smedes' terms, confusing 'unworthy' with 'undeserving'.[11]

I am convinced that many Christians fall into this error and are sure that because their fallibility leads them repeatedly into actions that need to be forgiven countless times, they are unworthy of the salvation that is offered to them. Grace is offered to us because we are of infinite value in the sight of our Lord who created us and in the person of Christ gave himself in love for us. Even though we do not deserve his love, we are deemed worthy to receive it, and we can rest assured of the love he gives us, while recognising and confessing the faults and weaknesses that constantly beset us. 'A person who has had a bath needs only to wash his feet', says Jesus (Jn 13.10).

'Be kind to yourself' was the advice given to me by a therapist in the 1990s when I suffered an acute crisis of self-confidence following numerous family and professional problems. When my beliefs deserted me for some years about ten years ago, I lost all sense of worthiness of receiving any grace at all, largely because I felt that I had tried so hard over so many years of belief and 'service' and had failed to achieve any goodness in the sight of God. I had confused worth with deserving.

Michael Henchard is so steeped in his own misery and wretchedness that he fails to recognise how much goodness actually is demonstrated in his nature and his actions. And the love and goodness that he shows before his death begets love in its turn. But such is his self-loathing that he is blinded to the knowledge of what goodness he shows, and blinded also to the possibility that he can be redeemed and forgiven by the 'Somebody' whose hand he is briefly aware of.

Our Lord, in his adaptation of the Ten Commandments, points to two central commandments, the second of which, as we know, is 'Love your neighbour as yourself' (Mt. 22.39, Mk 12.31, Lk. 10.27). Whereas the emphasis is often on the love of neighbour as distinct from the love for God highlighted in the first commandment, it is often overlooked that Jesus, with his knowledge of the human psyche and with some irony, is implying that if our love for our neighbour were to be anywhere near as great as our love for ourselves, then our neighbour would indeed be extremely well served. Jesus, in fact, is assuming the extent of our self-love. This is not selfishness, but a realistic understanding that we are made in God's image for a great purpose. We have much to be proud of in our humanity, as well as much to regret and confess. I believe that the prayer has the right balance which begins: 'Remember, O Lord, what you have wrought in us and not what we deserve.'

To conclude on a light note, in a little book that I keep at my bedside, *Winnie the Pooh's Little Book of Wisdom*, the heading on one page is:

Love your Neighbour as Yourself
'Oh Bear!' said Christopher Robin.
'How I do love you!'
'So do I', said Pooh.[12]

And that is how it should be.

This article was first published in *The Epworth Review*, October 2007.

Endnotes

1 Thomas Hardy, *The Mayor of Casterbridge* (London: Penguin, 1997), 320.
2 Hardy, *Casterbridge*, 295.
3 Hardy, *Casterbridge*, 301.
4 Hardy, *Casterbridge*, 320.
5 *Hymns and Psalms* (London: Methodist Publishing House, 1983), no. 215.
6 *Hymns and Psalms*, no. 226.
7 Hardy, *Casterbridge*, 307.
8 Lewis Smedes, *Shame and Grace* (London: SPCK, 1993), 80.
9 Smedes, *Shame*, 119.
10 Smedes, *Shame*, 120.
11 *The Observer*, 21.01.07, 5.
12 Published by Egmont Children's Books, London 1999.

Lifting the Curse
Reflections on retribution and restoration

The Fig-Tree

Jesus is hungry as he returns to the temple in Jerusalem that he had visited the day before. He sees a fig-tree that has nothing on it but leaves. When, according to Matthew, he says 'May you never bear fruit again', the fig-tree immediately withers (Mt. 21.18-22). The original account in Saint Mark has Jesus saying the same thing to the tree and returning the next day to find that it has withered. At this point his disciples believe that Jesus has cursed the tree (Mk 11.12-14, 20-21).

Jesus has already visited the temple and ejected those who were trading there. While in both gospels the cursing of the fig tree occurs after the incident in the temple, in Mark the clearing of the temple is sandwiched between the moment of cursing and the following day's discovery by the disciples that the tree has withered. Both gospels follow the same sequence of events, but there are some differences in emphasis in the actions and words of Jesus that occur at the time.

My intention in this study is to examine the importance of the curse not only in this incident, but through the Old Testament and in literature before the coming of Christ, and to suggest how Jesus lifts the curse of vengeance and retribution.

The Failure of Israel

The cursing and withering of the fig-tree have given rise to many different reactions, among them the serious doubt whether Jesus would ever have wanted the fig-tree to be cursed to bear no more fruit. And as Tom Wright points out echoing the feelings of sceptics, why blame the fig-tree when 'it wasn't yet time for figs; surely Jesus was being petty and petulant, cursing the tree for doing what fig trees always do, putting out leaves in the spring, but not yet bearing fruit'.[1] But, he also agrees, with many others, that the incident is inextricably linked with the clearing of the temple and with Jesus' condemnation of the traders and money-changers. One commentator points out that 'since Mark's custom is faithfully to report what he received and to tell stories as they happened [...] we are justified [...] in seeing in its starkness and destructiveness a solemn warning of what was in fact to happen in the destruction of Jerusalem in AD 70'.[2] When Jesus, on leaving the temple, is recorded by Mark as saying 'not one stone here will be left on another; every one will be thrown down' (Mk 13.2), it is as if Our Lord is making a factual statement about the future, as well as a judgement on Israel's past and present. D.E. Nineham also makes the point that the fate of the fig-tree symbolises the fate awaiting Jerusalem and the Jewish people and religion. 'Like the fig-tree with its leaves, the Jewish people made a fine show with their numerous ceremonies and outward observances, but when the Messiah came looking for the fruit of righteousness he found none, and the result was condemnation and destruction for Judaism, as it was for the tree.'[3]

According to R.A. Cole, 'this withering of the tree is only a perpetuation of its present fruitless condition'. Extending the withering of the fig tree to the withering of the temple as the symbol of the fruitless religion of Israel, Cole says that 'henceforth Israel was to be withered and fruitless; the physical judgement of AD 70 was only an outward sign of this'.[4] Recalling the words of Jesus in quoting from Isa. 56.7, 'My house will be called a house of prayer for all

134

nations', Cole says that for Jesus 'the supreme blasphemy was that this place, which was to have been in God's purpose a place of prayer for non-Jewish people of every nation, instead of being an exclusively Jewish national sanctuary, should have become a business-house, and for dishonest business at that'.[5]

While the emphasis in Mark has been shown to be on the importance of taking the news of salvation to the Gentiles, Matthew does not forget the mission to the Jews. Stanley Hauerwas, in his classic commentary *Matthew*, points out that 'Jesus' cleansing of the temple is not a rejection of the significance of the temple, rather it is an indication of its importance'. He continues: 'The God of Israel, the God worshipped in the temple, is the same God who is the father of Jesus, the Son. The people of Israel, the Jews, can never be "left behind" because if they are left behind Christians discover that we can make no sense of Jesus.'[6] The people of Israel have had to learn their lesson and heed the warning. This is expressed strongly by Wright when he considers the significance of Jesus' words on faith, visualising Jesus standing next to the mountain on which the temple stands and comparing the fate of the temple with that of the mountain which is thrown into the sea. The promise to the disciples, he says,

> Is not a general comment about the power of prayer to do extraordinary things […] The promise is far more focused than that. Saying to "this mountain" that it should be "lifted up and thrown into the sea" when you are standing right beside the Temple mountain, was bound to be taken as another coded warning about what would happen to the Temple as God's judgment fell upon his rebellious people.[7]

Such a warning certainly would increase the hostility of the authorities towards Jesus.

The warning to the Jews of their failure to live up to Jesus' mission to them has already been signalled in Our Lord's commission to his disciples to go to 'the lost sheep of the house of Israel' (Mt. 10.5-6) and in his encounter with the Canaanite woman when he tells her that his mission is 'only to the lost sheep of the house of Israel', though it is very probable that she is able to remind him of the needs of those other than the people of Israel (Mt. 15.24). Both Mark and Matthew record that at the time of the visit to the temple, Jesus tells us a parable of the tenants who kill the son of the owner of the vineyard in their desperate attempt to get control of the vineyard, with the strong implication that the words Jesus quotes from Ps. 118.22-23 that 'the stone the builders rejected has become the capstone' is a direct reference to the forthcoming rejection of Jesus by the Jews at whom his mission was originally directed (Mt. 21.42 and Mk 11.10). Matthew has a further brief parable at that point telling of two sons, one of whom rejects his father's commission to work in the vineyard, but then accepts, whereas the second does the exact opposite, indicating the failure of the Israelite people to carry out the covenant they had previously made with God (Mt. 21.28-31). Matthew's later parable of the wedding banquet further illustrates the way in which the favoured people fail to live up to the privilege of their invitation into the Kingdom: 'The wedding banquet is ready, but those I invited did not deserve to come' (Mt. 22.8). So the unlikeliest people are now invited. As had been said just previously 'I tell you, the tax collectors and the prostitutes are entering the Kingdom of God ahead of you' (Mt. 21.31). Such warnings fuel the authorities' resentment even further.

The Curse in the Old Testament

In the Old Testament the images of the withered vine and the fig-tree have signalled the failure of the people to fulfil the covenant and the promise to serve their God faithfully. Jeremiah says:

> I will take away their harvest, declares the Lord,
> There will be no grapes on the vine,

There will be no figs on the tree,
And their leaves will wither (Jer. 8.13).

And later in Jeremiah, he utters the dire prophecy of the Lord as follows: 'I will send the sword, famine and plague against them and I will make them like poor figs that are so bad they cannot be eaten' (Jer. 29.17). Morna Hooker draws our attention to three more important Old Testament references in which God is shown as looking in vain for the early figs and the prophet expresses intense disappointment at the results:[8]

> When I found Israel,
> it was like finding grapes in the desert;
> when I saw your fathers,
> it was like seeing the early fruit on the fig-tree,
> But when they came to Baar Peor,
> They consecrated themselves to that shameful idol
> And became as vile as the thing they loved (Hos. 9.10).

And just a few verses later:

> Ephraim is blighted,
> Their root is withered,
> They yield no fruit (Hos. 9.16).

In Micah, Israel's misery is reflected as follows:

> What misery is mine!
> I am like one who gathers summer fruit
> at the gleaning of the vineyard;
> there is no cluster of grapes to eat,
> none of the early figs that I crave (Mic. 7.1).

In Habakkuk, the prophet praises the Lord despite the state of the nation, as he admits, though the fig-tree does not bud

> And there are no grapes on the vines (Hab. 3.17).

Jonah, nursing his grievance that God has forgiven the citizens of Nineveh, is more concerned that the vine under which he is sheltering has withered than he is about the fate of Nineveh. When the Lord says to him: 'Should I not be concerned about that great city?', he is telling Jonah that the mission of believers should be opened up to those whom we have neglected, distrusted or ignored (Jon. 4.11). The message is that the people of Israel must enlarge their sympathies which have become withered and decayed.

While at the time of Jesus' dealings in the Temple Jesus links the curse with the withering of the fig-tree, God's curse played a very significant part in the early history of the human race as recorded in the opening chapters of Genesis. Because of his disobedience in succumbing to the wiles of Eve, Adam becomes a victim of the curse that will pursue him throughout his life:

> Cursed is the ground because of you;
> Through painful toil you will eat of it
> All the days of your life (Gen. 3.17).

According to Henri Blocher, the tree of the knowledge of good and evil in the Garden of Eden 'represents ingratitude and rebellion against God's provision, the absurd pretension to abolish dependence and the disastrous misuse of the privilege of being accountable to God'.[9] He sees this as a deliberate, moral 'breaking of the covenant' that God has given to Adam which 'defines [...] both the generosity of the Lord and the duties he imposes'(Gen. 2.15),[10] following the Lord's provision of the paradise of Eden and his call to Adam to cultivate it. Though one could assert that God had presumably created in Adam the free will to reject his call, the decision to do so lies at Adam's door, the consequence of the chain effect of the wiles of the manipulative serpent and Eve's weak surrender to temptation.

Adam is thus banished from the Garden of Eden 'to work the ground from which he had been taken' (Gen. 3.23). In the history of Cain and Abel, it is Cain who perpetuates the curse, following in Adam's footsteps as the tiller of the soil. When Abel keeps his flocks and Cain tills the soil, Cain kills his brother from jealousy. Before the murder, Cain has been clearly warned by the Lord of the difference between the right and the wrong course of action: 'If you do what is right will you not be accepted? But if you do not do what is right, sin is crouching at your door. It desires to have you, but you must master it' (Gen. 4.7), a warning that Cain deliberately ignores. His jealousy seems to have arisen because the Lord favours Abel's offering of fat portions of his flocks as against Cain's mere offering of soil. No other reason is suggested there than the Lord's greater pleasure in Abel's offering, which enrages Cain. In Heb. 4.11, a reason is given, namely that 'by faith Abel offered God a better sacrifice than Cain did'. When Cain kills his brother, he is told: 'Your brother's blood cries out to me from the ground. Now you are under a curse and driven from the ground, which opened its mouth to receive your brother's blood from your hand. When you work the ground, it will no longer yield its crops for you' (Gen. 4.10-11). By his deliberate choice Cain has brought the curse on himself.

In its full statement of the Law, Deuteronomy has it that a person is cursed for an entire series of moral infringements which are listed. These acts are entirely the fault of the individual caused through their own humanity and waywardness (Deut. 27.15-26), but they have already been prefaced by the statement that 'anyone who is hung on a tree is under God's curse' (Deut. 21.23), the punishment supposedly representing God's response to moral failure. This is echoed centuries later in the letter to the Galatians, which will be considered later.

The Greeks and the Curse

What is already emerging is a dual pattern. On the one hand, the curse seems to cling inexorably to successive generations of the chosen people who appear to be almost destined to fall into sin; but on the other hand it is clear that these lapses are caused through their own fault, their personal failures of jealousy, greed or lust. This pattern finds its parallel in the most important literature of the time before the birth of Christ, in the Greek tragedians, from whose works a few examples may be drawn.

One classical scholar, Charles Seltman, considering forces outside human control, distinguishes between sin and guilt when he writes:

> Clearly the only sin was to commit a personal offence against a divinity. As for guilt, like the guilt of Oedipus or of Orestes, that was altogether a different matter; it had been put upon you by a Fate beyond the gods, and there was nothing for it but to be purified by a god. It was dire misfortune, but no fault of yours.[11]

This is supported by the theologian John Austin Baker, who writes: 'Here the idea of Destiny as the ultimate ruler comes into play. Neither are the gods exempt from Fate themselves, nor are they able to deliver their protégés.'[12] However, Oedipus himself in Sophocles' *King Oedipus*, in his long speech when he is confronted with the truth of his murder of his father both admits his responsibility 'On me is the curse that none but I have laid', and yet almost immediately places the blame on a god elsewhere:

> Can it be any but some monstrous god
> Of evil that has sent this doom upon me?[13]

This sin against a god as his personal responsibility is confirmed later when he says to the chorus:

> Apollo, friends, Apollo
> Has laid this agony upon me;
> Not by his hand; I did it.[14]

This is confirmed a little later when he accepts full responsibility for his crime.

He says to the chorus:

> Touch me, and have no fear. On no man else
> But on me alone is the scourge of my punishment.[15]

However, in his conversation with the chorus in *Oedipus at Colonus*, he denies responsibility: 'Nothing was of my choosing',[16] and justifies his action:

> He whom I killed
> Had sought to kill me first.[17]

And he attributes this to 'an ancient grudge/against our house', saying:

> If my father was foredoomed
> By the voice of heaven to die by his own son's hand,
> How can you justly cast it against *me*,
> Who was still unborn when the decree was spoken?[18]

This brings us back very much to Seltman's contention that there is a higher, supernatural power, 'a fate beyond the gods', whom one can never overcome.

The attribution of responsibility to sources outside oneself is found elsewhere in Greek tragedy. In Euripides' *Hippolytus*, Phaedra blames her mother for her own shameful passion for her stepson, Hippolytus, that rages within her and also destroys her sister, refusing to accept her own responsibility for her feelings: 'I believe that such misfortune does not arise from inborn folly, since often those who suffer are wise and good'.[19] In *Agamemnon*, Clytemnestra even blames their daughter, Iphigenia, who, she says, causes the death of Agamemnon and Cassandra although it is Agamemnon who murders his own daughter, Iphigenia:

> That Fury,
> She steered the blade
> Through Agamemnon,
> Not I. Not my hand.
> The hand of our daughter
> Iphigenia
> Steadied the hand
> Of that Fury.[20]

She has just highlighted 'the curse, the hideous/Heritage/of the house of Atreus' that had been clinging to generations of the family, thus shifting the responsibility even further back than the innocent Iphigenia. Aegisthus, her lover, in the final scene of the play narrates the full history of the feud in the house of Atreus, a seemingly unbreakable chain of evil extending through generations. Once Clytemnestra has had her revenge on her husband, she tries to call a halt to the slaughter: 'Stop. Stop/The killing is over',[21] but we know that she in turn is killed by her son, Orestes, in *Choephori*. However, in the third play of the trilogy, *The Eumenides*, the goddess Athene, speaking with the reasonableness of Athenian values, heals the situation and banishes the curse through sweet reason and the force of argument:

> The sacred power of persuasion
> That makes calm the storm in the body,
> The presence of God in persuasion
> Draws the poison fangs of evil.[22]

The exercise of the power of reason may be convincing to a certain degree, but does not, I believe, meet the deep and powerful emotions that urge human beings to exact vengeance on those who, they believe, have wronged them. In the final scene of *Choephori*, the chorus, having summarised the course of the chain of evil cause and effect thus far, ask the all-important questions:

> Can the poor, scorched brains of Orestes
> Figure out all the factors? Can he solve
> The arithmetic of the unfinished
> That shunts this curse from one generation to the next?
> Who can bring it to an end?
> When can it be brought to an end?
> How can it be brought to an end?[23]

Sow and Reap

While in light of the coming of Christ a greater answer has been made available, at this stage in the experience and thought of the Greeks, at least willpower is needed to achieve what reason cannot. It is clear that, had Oedipus controlled his temper when confronted by the brutality of Laius, his father, on the road, he would not have murdered him. Similarly, Cain has only to control his jealousy and temper to prevent the death of his brother. In the final play of Sophocles' trilogy, *Antigone,* the blind Teiresias summarises the situation even before the final tragedies have occurred:

> You cannot alter this. The gods themselves
> Cannot undo it. It follows of necessity
> From what you have done.[24]

Evil consequences arise from our human actions and even higher powers cannot change the course of events. And when one considers that, as H.D.F. Kitto says, 'to requite one's foes with harm was normal Greek ethics',[25] the problem is rather removed from the jurisdiction of the gods. Kitto further says, this time in relation to Creon in *Antigone*: 'The gods are angry with Creon, their Erinyes will punish him; yet the punishment […] on Creon as it were automatically, out of what he himself has done. The gods are not directing events from the outside; they work in the events.'[26]

Hence, while the responsibility lies with the individual for the freewill decision to respond in kind, the Greeks see the ultimate cause to be within the hands of the gods who have implanted such desires within the hearts of their protagonists.

If we return to the Scriptures, we find that they too give warnings of human responsibility for events, but the responsibility for evil acts is placed firmly within the hearts of humankind following the freewill decisions recorded in Genesis. Job is warned by one of his three friends, Eliphaz:

As I have observed, those who plough evil
And those who sow trouble reap it (Job 4.8).

And this is reiterated in Proverbs:

He who sows wickedness reaps trouble,
And the rod of his fury will be destroyed (Prov. 22.8).

In the New Testament, too, Paul expresses the same thought when he writes: 'Do not be deceived. God cannot be mocked. A man reaps what he sows. The one who sows to please his sinful nature, from that nature will reap destruction' (Gal. 6.7).

In that most popular of morality tales, Dickens' *A Christmas Carol*, the ghost of Jacob Marley, Scrooge's partner who had died seven years previously that Christmas Eve and who now appears to him in chains, tells Scrooge that he, Marley, also reaped what he had sown: 'I wear the chain I forged in life [...] I made it link by link, and yard by yard; I girded it on of my own free will, and of my own free will I wore it.'[27] This is reiterated later in the story by Scrooge's nephew when, accompanied by the Ghost of Christmas Present, Scrooge overhears the comment about himself: 'His offences carry their own punishment.'[28]

The conclusion that our actions result directly from our own failures brings us back to the fig-tree in another brief allusion in Proverbs: 'He who tends a fig-tree will eat its fruit' (Prov. 27.18). We must bear the consequences of our actions. The same spirit of divine retribution is expressed in 1 Corinthians: 'Don't you know that you are God's temple and that God's Spirit lives in you? If anyone destroys God's temple, God will destroy him' (1 Cor. 3.16-17).

There is a law of cause and effect which means that a person's actions have automatic consequences. In Blocher's words when he reviews the curse on Adam, man 'turns a garden into a desert'.[29] This is a foretaste of the response of Jesus in cursing the fig-tree that represents the history of Israel's persistent faithlessness and failure despite God's love and purpose for the nation. The ultimate responsibility for the evil lies in the human psyche, as, when recording the words of Jesus, the down-to-earth Mark argues:

> What comes out of a man is what makes him
> "unclean". For from within, out of men's hearts,
> come evil thoughts, sexual immorality, theft, murder,
> adultery, greed, malice, deceit, lewdness, envy, slander,
> arrogance and folly. All these evils come from inside
> and make a man "unclean" (Mk 7.20-23).

What arises out of this consideration of the relative importance of the curse of fate and human responsibility is the realisation that, while the characters involved in the chain of cause and effect see themselves as victims of the build-up of inescapable generational conflict, the choice in biblical terms lies within themselves and this chain can be broken by an exercise of willpower over the forces raging within us.

Lifting the Curse

However, while the Greeks saw an inscrutable fate that presided over and intervened in human fortunes, controlling human responses, Christians, while holding that behaviour is dependant on an exercise of free will, also believe that the 'curse' can be lifted by divine forces that do not depend on human responses for their fulfilment. In other words, God can act on the events in question and change the entire emphasis from the negative one of retribution to the positive course of restoration.

If we now return to the time of Adam and Eve's disobedience in the Garden of Eden, we find that, despite their disobedience and the suffering that Eve will endure in child-bearing, 'the Lord God made garments of skin for Adam and his wife and clothed them' (Gen. 3.21). God allows his children his protection and he ensures their preservation, but they continue in a limbo, in what Dietrich Bonhoeffer describes as 'twilight', a state between good and evil, wanting life yet held in a spiritual death, 'beyond God's good'.[30] Earlier in the same work Bonhoeffer has said:

> In this fate under the curse […] humankind is given the promise of victory, a victory that has to be fought for and has to be won again and again, but one in which it tramples the serpent's head underfoot. To be sure, this battle leaves humankind wounded, for the serpent, though defeated, still bites it in the heel […] It is this sort of battle, which humankind takes upon itself as curse and as promise and in which it fights to the end, that it is allowed to live.[31]

God is in the final analysis unable to cease to be a God of love: he will always allow his children, even though he is angry with them, a possible way through with his protection. Similarly, when Cain has slain his brother, come under God's curse and fears that he will be driven from the land as a punishment to become 'a restless wanderer on the face of the earth', 'the Lord put a mark on Cain so that no-one who found him would kill him' even though they would know and recognise him (Gen. 4.13-15). And Noah and his family, despite the faithlessness of their race, are given the Lord's protection from the Flood in the covenant, the sign of which is the rainbow, a recurring symbol of God's presence and favour towards Noah (Gen. 9.12-16). The promise of God's favour as a prospect for the faithful is expressed later in Micah when, as an echo of Jonah's attempt to find shelter under his vine, Micah tells of God's blessing when 'the mountain of the Lord's temple will be established' (Mic. 4.1). A few verses later he says:

> Every man will sit under his own vine
> and under his own fig-tree,
> and no-one will make them afraid,
> for the Lord Almighty has spoken (Mic. 4.4).

The complete picture is rather that of an enormous coin, one side of which depicts God's anger with disobedience and our failure to live up to his standards, while the other side depicts his mercy which, while he knows our persistent frailty, refuses to abandon his creation. A prime example of the Lord's grace to the penitent is found in David's confession after his heinous crime in sending Bathsheba's husband, Uriah, out into the front line to his certain death:

> Have mercy on me, O God,
> According to your unfailing love;
> According to your great compassion
> Blot out my transgressions.
> Wash away all my iniquity
> And cleanse me from my sin.
> For I know my transgressions,
> And my sin is always before me.
> Against you, you only, have I sinned
> And done evil in your sight (Ps. 51.1-4).

Such is the depth of David's remorse and acknowledgement of his sin that he is restored to the Lord's great love and purpose for him. Such grace anticipates the saving, sacrificial love of Christ through the Cross and also clearly defines what we have already seen in God's promise to cover and protect Adam and his descendants.

While in the clearing of the temple and the withering of the fig-tree, Jesus shows his anger with Israel, Luke uses the fig-tree in his parable of the vine grower and the man who looks after the vineyard for him. Whereas the fig-tree is constantly unfruitful and the owner wants to cut it down, the other man pleads for him to allow the tree just one more year to give it the chance to make amends and bear fruit: 'If it bears fruit next year, fine! If not, then cut it down' (Lk. 13.9). And who knows how many more chances the man would have allowed the fig-tree in his refusal to give up on it? And while in Mark and Matthew Jesus is displeased with the evidence that there are no figs but only leaves on the tree that he curses, both evangelists use the leaves of the fig tree in a very positive context later when looking ahead to the future of the Kingdom of God. 'Now learn this lesson from the fig-tree: As soon as its twigs get tender and its leaves come out, you know that summer is near' (Mk 13.28). Matthew repeats this in the same words (Mt. 24.32).

While it is clear that God provides a redemptive antidote to the poison of the curse, it is also important to see the response that his people are commanded to make.

We are not to be merely passive, though grateful recipients of his promises and grace,but to make a definite, clear response of obedience to his commands. As early as in Leviticus, the command is clear: 'Do not hate your brother in your heart. Rebuke your neighbour frankly, so that you will not share in his guilt. Do not seek revenge or bear a grudge against one of your people, but love your neighbour as yourself. I am the Lord' (Lev.19.17-18).

This is echoed with the full authority of the life and character of Jesus in the recorded sayings of the Sermon on the Mount when Our Lord says: 'You have heard that it was said "Love your neighbour and hate your enemy". But I tell you: Love your enemies and pray for those who persecute you, that you may be sons of your Father in heaven' (Mt. 5.43-44). Not only are we commanded to avoid revenge, but also to make the positive move of love towards those who would harm us, to go the extra mile, to turn the other cheek. Stanley Hauerwas extends these injunctions from the personal to the wider context of the political struggles between groups and nations, emphasising the very topical importance of applying the teachings of Our Lord to the relationships between factions and religious groups today:

> If we do not learn to forgive then we will not be
> forgiven, we will not be part of the [...] new people
> brought into existence by Jesus. To forgive and to be
> forgiven is not some crude exchange bargain to "get
> on with life", but rather to participate in a political
> alternative that ends our attempts to secure our
> existence through violence.[32]

But we are not only called upon to make the monumental effort to cease from violence and to forgive what may in the past have seemed to be unforgiveable. There has to be a process of dying to the past and being resurrected to new life so that the past is extinguished. As Jesus is recorded as saying in some vivid images: 'No-one sews a patch of unshrunk cloth on an old garment. If he does, the new piece will pull away from the old, making the tear worse. And no-one pours new wine into old wineskins. If he does, the wine will burst the skins, and both the wine and the wineskins will be ruined. No, he pours new wine into new wineskins' (Mk 2.21-22).

This renewal can only be found in a complete break with the past: our tendency simply to attempt to patch up broken relationships and situations is not sufficiently radical and will fail. When at the trial of Jesus, the people say that they are prepared to 'let his blood be on us and on our children' (Mt. 27.25). Our Lord's answer from the cross is: 'Forgive them, for they do not know what they are doing' (Lk. 23.34). When Jesus forgives those who crucify him, he is offering the same forgiveness to us and all people, for without his forgiveness all our efforts to reverse the curse of retribution will be of no effect. We must repent, receive forgiveness when our past and our failings are cancelled, and then we can make a new start.

Jesus forgives us, when the authorities, rather than stoning him to death as was the normal punishment in such cases, want him crucified in what was the cruellest death of all, not simply to kill him, but to fulfil the words in Deut. 21.23 that anyone who is hanged on a tree is accursed. John Austin Baker suggests the reasons why the authorities wanted Jesus crucified rather than stoned:

> They particularly wanted Jesus to die in the way he
> did; and for that their most probable motive is to
> be found in the declaration in the Jewish Law, that
> everyone who is hanged (a term taken at this period to
> include crucifixion) is accursed of God (Deut. 21.23).

> They wanted to make it clear to everyone for all time
> that this man's teaching and pretensions were utterly
> rejected by God.[33]

To all appearances, the death of Christ must have been for the disciples a total failure and defeat, even a curse visited upon their new faith. It must have seemed ironical to the disciples that he who had cursed the failure of the nation of Israel should now be sharing the same curse. Paul emphasises this in Galatians when, in transforming the reference in Deut. 21.23 that 'cursed is everyone who is hung on a tree', he sees Christ as bearing the entire curse of the sins of the nation of Israel and of the world: 'Christ redeemed us from the curse of the law by becoming a curse for us' (Gal. 3.13). It is small wonder that his disciples, not understanding what they witness on Calvary, are defeated and slink away into hiding.

The raising of Christ from the dead transforms the situation from an apparent defeat into a victory over death and our human frailty and sin. In Paul's first letter to the Corinthians he asks the questions, when writing about the resurrection of the dead: 'How are the dead raised? With what kind of body will they come?'. He then answers his own questions with the apparently puzzling remark which moves the focus back to events before the resurrection: 'How foolish! What you sow does not come to life unless it dies' (1 Cor. 15.35-36). Nothing can be resurrected unless it had already died. And this brings us back to the important point that the lifting of the curse and restoration must begin with a death, the death of the old self, the old ethics of retribution and curse in which Jesus, in cursing the fig-tree, is apparently partaking, but which he is soon to annul through his own death. When Jesus, as recorded in John's Gospel, tells his disciples that his hour has come, he mysteriously deploys the image of a seed falling into the ground, illustrating not defeat but how he will be glorified: 'The hour has come for the Son of Man to be glorified. I tell you the truth, unless a grain of wheat falls to the ground and dies, it remains only a single seed. But if it dies, it produces many seeds' (Jn 12.24).

The point has already been made vividly in the same letter to the Corinthians when death is equated with Adam and his disobedience, and life is found in Christ: 'For as in Adam all die, so in Christ all will be made alive' (1 Cor. 15.22). The proclamation that this life is offered to all takes the message of salvation out into the world beyond Israel, just as when at the death of Christ the temple veil is torn down the middle, the Good News, at the moment of its most apparent nadir, is opened up to all peoples.

So the curse has been lifted. Christ has achieved this and it is the Holy Spirit that makes this available for all people throughout all ages. It needs Christ's forgiveness and the cancellation of our sin and the curse so that a new beginning can happen. It demands a rejection of retribution and revenge, an end to retributive violence, the death of the ego that demands satisfaction for wrongs, real and imaginary. And it demands a belief that the fig leaves which are thought to promise nothing may indeed be the messengers of a new and promising future of reconciliation and regeneration.

This article was first published in *The European Journal of Theology*, January 2013.

Endnotes

1 Tom Wright, *Mark for Everyone* (London: SPCK 2001), 150.

2 D. English, *The Message of Mark* (Leicester: Inter-Varsity Press, 1992), 189.

3 D.E. Nineham, *St Mark* (London: Penguin, 1963), 299.

4 R.A. Cole, *Mark* (Leicester: Tyndale New Testament Commentaries, Inter-Varsity Press, 1989), 250.

5 Cole, *Mark*, 252.

6 Stanley Hauerwas, *Matthew* (London: SCM Press, 2006), 187

7 Tom Wright, *Matthew for Everyone* (London: SPCK, 2002), 72-73.

8 Morna Hooker, *The Gospel According to St Mark* (London: A. & C. Black, 1991), 261.

9 Henri Blocher, *In the Beginning: The Opening Chapters of Genesis* (Nottingham: Inter-Varsity Press, 1984), 133.

10 Blocher, *Beginning*, 112.

11 Charles Seltman, *The Twelve Olympians* (London: Pan Books, 1952), 23.

12 J.A. Baker, *The Foolishness of God* (London: Darton, Longman and Todd 1970), 23.

13 Sophocles, *King Oedipus*, from *The Theban Plays*, translated by E.F. Watling (London: Penguin, 1947), 48.

14 Sophocles, *Oedipus*, 62.

15 Sophocles, *Oedipus*, 64.

16 Sophocles, *Oedipus at Colonus*, from *The Theban Plays* (London: Penguin, 1947), 87.

17 Sophocles, *Colonus*, 88.

18 Sophocles, *Colonus*, 101.

19 Euripides, *Hippolytus*, from *Alcestis and Other Plays*, translated by Philip Vellacott (London: Penguin,1953), 39.

20 Aeschylus, *Agamemnon,* from the *Oresteia*, translated by Ted Hughes (London: Faber & Faber, 1999), 75.

21 Aeschylus, *Agamemnon*, 83.

22 Aeschylus, *The Eumenides*, from *The Oresteia*, translated by Ted Hughes (London: Faber & Faber,1999), 191.

23 Aeschylus, *Choephori*, from *The Oresteia*, translated by Ted Hughes (London: Faber & Faber, 1999), 143.

24 Sophocles, *Antigone*, from *The Theban Plays* (London: Penguin 1953), 155.

25 H.D.F. Kitto, *Greek Tragedy* (London and New York: Routledge, 1966), 79.

26 Kitto, *Greek Tragedy*, 127-128.

27 Charles Dickens, *A Christmas Carol and Other Writings* (London: Penguin, 2003), 47-48.

28 Dickens, *Christmas Carol*, 87.

29 Blocher, *Beginning*, 184.

30 Dietrich Bonhoeffer, *Creation and Fall*, translated by Douglas Stephen Bax (Minneapolis: Fortress Press, 1997), 140.

31 Bonhoeffer, *Creation*, 133.

32 Hauerwas, *Matthew*, 79. Also in Matt. 9.17 and Lk. 5.37.

33 Baker, *Foolishness*, 183.

The Remembering Self
Reflections on reconciliation and its absence

Seeking Revenge

Two elderly gentlemen are sitting facing each other at dinner. There is one empty seat at the table, which should have been occupied by the dead wife of the host, the General. She has been dead for 33 years. The other man, a fellow officer, had been his best friend in their childhood and youth. They are estranged, because the General has reasons to believe that the other man had had an affair with his wife and had tried to shoot him in a hunting 'accident'. The General has waited for 41 years for this encounter. They have not seen each other in the meantime. The General wants to know the truth. This confrontation is his notion of revenge. Though the truth emerges, there is no confession, no forgiveness and no reconciliation.

In this study we consider why confrontation leading to revenge so often excludes forgiveness and reconciliation. We will also consider the conditions for reconciliation and will study examples from biblical and other literature. Finally, we will attempt to see how God's answer supersedes our human systems.

The events described above occur in the novel, *Embers*, by the Hungarian novelist, Sandor Marai.[1] Since the events of the hunting expedition and the following day when it transpires that the General's wife, Krisztina, has been betraying him with Konrad, his best friend, the General does not speak to Krisztina for eight years. He lives apart from her until she dies. His solitude has allowed him to nurture his grievance and to retain his exact memory of events. He is guided solely by the prospect of revenge and has set himself decisively against any prospect of forgiveness. His desire for vengeance is driven by the destruction of the trust and friendship built up between them since childhood. 'If a man gives someone his trust [...] because of that blind, unconditional devotion, which is the highest thing any one person can offer another, only then to witness the faithlessness and base behaviour of his friend, is he permitted to rise up in protest and demand vengeance?'[2] The answer to his rhetorical question is yes. He counters the reader's unspoken accusation of vanity: 'Vanity, you say. Yes, vanity [...] and yet self-respect is what gives a person his or her intrinsic value.'[3] He has a mixture of good and bad reasons to justify his hatred and to turn friendship into a desire for revenge.

The psychologist, Steven Pinker, has the phrase 'the Moralization Gap'[4] to describe the way in which antagonists become entrenched in their opposing positions, where there is a 'difference between the way people judge other people's behaviour and the way they judge their own' as a 'self-serving bias'. He continues: 'Each side sincerely believes its version of the story, namely that it is an innocent and long-suffering victim and the other side a malevolent and treacherous sadist.'[5] Later he talks of 'the dimmer switch for revenge'[6] when the offender falls within our natural circle of empathy, or the relationship with the perpetrator has become too valuable to sever. However, the previous friendship and the betrayal by his wife, Krisztina, have only intensified the General's hatred and desire for revenge. Pinker's view does not always allow for the fact that intense hatred can be the reverse of the coin of intense love. At one point during the General's honeymoon, they are the guests of an Arab and witness the killing of a lamb. Krisztina turns pale, understanding that, as the General explains to Konrad, 'in Hungarian our words for killing and embracing echo and heighten each other'.[7]

Remembering

Memory clearly serves to intensify the desire for revenge. The General confirms this: 'With age, memory enlarges every detail and presents it in the sharpest outline.'[8] However, it seems that memory is not only the means of feeding revenge, but has been described as the essential precondition of reconciliation. Emmanuel Katangole and Chris Rice criticise what they call 'reconciliation without memory [...] that ignores the wounds of the world and proclaims peace where there is no peace.'[9] This is developed as 'jumping over the past too quickly by offering cheap grace to those who have done wrong and never repented.'[10] Even if the General had been prepared to forgive and seek reconciliation with his former friend, Konrad does not repent, and in fact hardly utters a word in response to the General's accurate speculations about the events so long ago. The meeting ends without reconciliation, but Konrad's failure to deny the accusations and his acknowledgement of their truth are convincing enough. The fact that Nini, the General's old servant, observes early on that the General already knows the truth does not deter him from confronting Konrad with the results of his haunted speculations with the intention of humiliating him with the memory of past evil.[11]

In his book, *Thinking, Fast and Slow*, Daniel Kahneman speaks of 'the remembering self' which he contrasts with 'the experiencing self'. He writes: 'The experiencing self does not have a voice. The remembering self is sometimes wrong, but it is the one that keeps score and governs what we learn from living, and it is the one that makes decisions. What we learn from the past is to maximise the qualities of our future memories. This is the tyranny of the remembering self.'[12] Memory can be extremely positive and creative: 'Memory [...] holds the vast repository of skills we have acquired in a lifetime of practice, which automatically produce adequate solutions to challenges as they arise.'[13] But a good sequence of experienced events can be marred by one negative incident, as he says in describing the experience of enjoying listening to a symphony on record only to find that the complete pleasure is ruined by a bad scratch at the conclusion. This final scratch can colour one's memory of the whole of the preceding events, as happens with the General, his wife and his best friend. It is the remembering self that dominates. And as stated above, the remembering self, essential for true reconciliation, can however be a force for the nurturing of bitterness and vengeful hatred as well as for constructive peacemaking and thus can warp, even destroy the personality.

Following Cain's vengeful murder of his brother, the record is only of regret for his actions, and then only because of God's punishment that he will be 'a restless wanderer on the earth' (Gen. 4.12).[14] And in the parable of the Lost Son, another account of fratricidal resentment, the elder son's resentment of his younger brother is governed by his memory of the latter's disgraceful behaviour, what he sees as his dubiously insincere and self-seeking motivation in returning home, by the fact that nobody has thought of alerting him to the prodigal's return and of the father's lavish treatment of him. While the father's response confirms that everything he has is available for the elder brother to enjoy, we never learn whether there is a reconciliation between the two brothers. Reconciliation depends on the free decision of the individuals concerned and if one of them cannot be reconciled, then it will not happen. The father's grace, which is the point of the parable, though vital, is not directly relevant in the case of reconciliation which must be between the two brothers confronting each other, though the father's interceding and encouragement would presumably help the process. This intervention is fully implied by Stanley Hauerwas who refers to Jesus' washing of his disciples' feet as an example of humility in setting an example of grace: 'But the loss of Christian structures and institutions makes it all the more important that the gentle care exemplified by Jesus in washing his disciples' feet [...] be unapologetically a witness to the One who would save us through the cross'.[15]

It certainly seems that if left to human nature, reconciliation is difficult to achieve and the intervention of the grace and love of God is essential. But it is not as if reconciliation with others is impossible in the mind of Christ who gives his blessing to the peacemakers (Mt. 5.9) and tells us that, if we have any grievance against our brother, we must first be reconciled to him, thus with hindsight chastising Cain and anticipating a severe criticism of the Prodigal's elder brother (Mt. 5.24). Jesus certainly does not regard reconciliation as an illusory ideal, but it has to be achieved through graft and self-sacrifice.

Anthony Bash maintains that, while person-to-person forgiveness, with the need for the full implementation of his three principles of 'confession, repentance and restitution' resulting in justice for the victim[16] 'can never be entirely just because the fact of the wrongdoing cannot be reversed', God's forgiveness is absolute as 'an expression of the atonement, in which wrongdoing and its effects are annihilated'.[17] The General in *Embers* is not demanding restitution, which would now be impossible, but simply 'the truth'. Bash also points out that when Christ speaks words of forgiveness from the Cross, the words are 'a prayer that *God* will forgive, not Jesus'.[18] God, as the First Person of the Trinity, has the prerogative of being able to forgive absolutely, and Jesus, though he says 'I and the Father are one' (Jn 10.30), defers to Him. We now need to consider more closely how reconciliation may be achieved and our part in this.

Atonement and Reconciliation

This reconciliation is stated most clearly in 2 Cor. 5.11-21. When God 'reconciled us to himself in Christ, not counting their sins against them', he is cancelling out our sins and preparing the way for us to accept forgiveness, new life and reconciliation with himself (2 Cor. 5.19). Bash emphasises that the phrase 'in Christ' shows that we are one with Christ and that 'because God forgives, so Christians, who are in Christ, can also forgive as God forgives'.[19] In 'not counting their sins against them', God has remembered the accumulated sin of the human race before him. But he has also committed to us the task of bringing reconciliation to the world and helping in the task of reconciling the world to God, so that we are 'Christ's ambassadors, as though God were making his appeal through us' (2 Cor. 5.20). In a previous work, Bash elegantly states our role in this: 'The capacity to forgive interpersonally is a correlate of having experienced divine forgiveness because [...] forgiveness is regenerative, enabling the recipient to become a forgiving person.'[20] We are enabled, as believers and members of the family of Christ, to be brought into the task of reconciliation through the power of God's love working through us, as Bash further says: 'The effect of receiving and experiencing God's forgiveness is to transform a person so that they develop a predisposition to forgive others.'[21] God's forgiving spirit settles in our hearts and becomes part of our very selves.

Returning to the parable of the Lost Son, we see another image of how atonement works. While it is clear that Jesus occupies the role of the forgiving Father, Henri Nouwen, in a very telling way of encapsulating God's work of atonement, indicates further that in the parable Jesus is 'the younger son without being rebellious. He is the elder son without being resentful. In everything he is obedient to the Father, but never his slave. He hears everything the Father says, but this does not make him his servant. He does everything the Father sends him to do, but remains completely free.'[22] This is true reconciliation when God himself is identified with all the characters in the events and unites them all in his love on the Cross. The Marxist scholar, Terry Eagleton, makes a very apposite comment on the way Christians view the atonement:

> The good accept evil by embracing it in their love and
> mercy. In taking it upon themselves, however, they are
> drawn inexorably into its orbit. The tragic scapegoat is
> a case in point. Christ [...] may not have been sinful,
> but Saint Paul observes that he was 'made sin' for the

sake of humanity. A redeemer must know in his bones
what he is redeeming […] Otherwise the situation
cannot be salvaged from the inside, which is the only
form of salvation that works.[23]

Only the power of God entering into our human frame in Jesus and
demonstrating his love and capability of bearing the weight of all
human suffering and sin can achieve the reconciliation that the world
so desperately needs.

Thus the possibility is there for reconciliation to be grasped
by the human race. While, according to Wolfhart Pannenberg,
'when a mission has seized a man so unconditionally, he no longer
has any choice with respect to that mission. He reserves no inner
independence for himself over against his mission', the freedom to
exercise one's independence as a fully human, autonomous person in
God's image must surely be retained in any act of forgiveness leading
to full reconciliation.[24] It is our human fallibility that paralyses us, in
the attempt to gain our own advantage, our pride, our desire to save
face, whether personally or as a nation or group. Often, the more
passionate we are in our allegiance to our cause, the harder it is for
us to bend our wills to the need for reconciliation. The General in
Embers says early on in the novel that his obsession with retaliation
has destroyed what faith he had: 'A man who has signed away his soul
and his fate to solitude is incapable of faith.'[25] He has become locked
in on himself and his obsession and blinded to any alternative. But
his tragedy is that once he has Konrad at his mercy and is questioning
him over the events, presenting his own well-founded speculations to
him, he realises the absolute futility of his revenge:

> Beyond words is the reality that Krisztina is dead –
> and we are still alive. When I understood this, it was
> already too late. All that was left was the waiting and
> the thirst for revenge – and now that the waiting is
> over and the time for revenge is here, I am amazed
> to feel how hopeless it all is, and the pointlessness of

anything we could learn or admit or fight out between
us.[26]

He had waited in vain for his wife to break silence and ask for his forgiveness. He had been too proud to go to her himself, and he only learned from his servant Nini on the day of the dinner confrontation that Krisztina had asked for him on her deathbed. He had missed so many opportunities of creating a reconciliation with the woman he had never ceased to love. Forty-one years of his life have been wasted in the solitary nurturing of a revenge that has led to nothing.

The contributions of some non-theologians that have been included in this study demonstrate the singular importance of reconciliation to the world in general, not only to people of faith. It is good that many have found it possible, in the power of God's love to forgive and create reconciliation with those who have murdered family members, and this must be our continued hope. Through reconciliation which does not happen in a void and where past grievances and hatreds must be remembered, confessed, repented of, then cancelled, the world must move into a future where revenge dims into forgiveness and acceptance so that Christ's words from the Cross: 'Father, forgive them, because they do not know what they are doing' (Lk. 23.34) may resonate through a world in which conflicts are resolved.

This article was first published in *Theology*, May/June 2015.

Endnotes

1 Sandor Marai, *Embers*, translated by Carol Brown Janeway (London: Penguin, 2003).

2 Marai, *Embers*, 129.

3 Marai, *Embers*, 223.

4 Steven Pinker, *The Better Angels of our Nature* (London: Penguin Allen Lane, 2011), 490.

5 Pinker, *Better Angels*, 492. Author's italics.

6 Pinker, *Better Angels*, 541.

7 Marai, *Embers*, 147. The author in his footnote gives the two words Ölés and ölelés.

8 Marai, *Embers*, 158.

9 Emmanuel Katangole and Chris Rice, *Reconciling All Things* (Downers Grove, IL: Inter-Varsity Press, 2008), 28.

10 Katangole and Rice, *Reconciling*, 33.

11 Marai, *Embers*, 85.

12 Daniel Kahneman, *Thinking, Fast and Slow* (London: Penguin, 2011), 381.

13 Kahneman, *Thinking*, 416.

14 Biblical references are to the New International Version.

15 Stanley Hauerwas and Jean Vanier, *Living Gently in a Violent World* (Downers Grove, IL: Inter-Varsity Press, 2008) in Hauerwas' chapter 'The Politics of Gentleness', 99.

16 Anthony Bash, *Just Forgiveness* (London: SPCK 2011), 22.

17 Bash, *Just Forgiveness*, 141.

18 Bash, *Just Forgiveness*, 141.

19 Bash, *Just Forgiveness*, 141

20 Anthony Bash, *Forgiveness and Christian Ethics* (Cambridge University Press, 2007), 100.

21 Bash, *Forgiveness*, 104.

22 Henri Nouwen, *The Return of the Prodigal Son* (London: Darton, Longman & Todd, 1992), 126.

23 Terry Eagleton, *On Evil* (Yale: Yale University Press, 2010), 56.

24 Wolfhart Pannenberg, *Jesus – God and Man*, translated by L.L. Wilkins and D.A. Priebe (London: SCM Press, 2002), 402.

25 Marai, *Embers*, 121.

26 Marai, *Embers*, 226.

'Last Year's Nests' and 'This Year's Birds'

Reflections on re-reading Graham Greene's *Monsignor Quixote* and some famous antecedents

The Italian Bishop

> A priest who can set before an unexpected guest good wine, good cheese and a remarkable steak is a priest who can hold his own in the highest of circles. We are here to bring sinners to repentance and there are more sinners among the bourgeois than among peasants. I would like you to go forth like your ancestor Don Quixote on the high roads of the world.[1]

These are the words of the Italian Bishop of Motopo whose Mercedes has broken down on the road near El Toboso in the region of la Mancha in Graham Greene's novel, *Monsignor Quixote*. It is the home of the local priest Father Quixote who has stopped to help him and then invited the Bishop back to his humble house and made him extremely welcome by giving him a meal with good wine.

In contrast to Father Quixote's bishop who fails to appreciate his qualities and is deeply sceptical of the assumption that Father Quixote is the descendant of Cervantes' famous hero, the Italian Bishop is generous and liberal and sees potential in Father Quixote. Father

Quixote is a humble and kind priest, living very frugally yet still able to donate money to a good cause that his Bishop finds very dubious, *In Vinculis* ('In Chains'), supported by the local Communist mayor and dedicated to helping prisoners. He owns an old Seat motor car which he regards with the same affection as his famous ancestor regarded his faithful steed and which he has also christened Rocinante. He does not consider himself well qualified in theology, having graduated at Madrid University rather than the more distinguished Salamanca, but devotes himself to serving the basic needs of his parishioners of whom he admits 'I don't teach them, they teach me' (74).

The Italian bishop has appreciated Father Quixote's warm hospitality and perceived that the priest needs to launch out into new ventures and realise his undoubted talents. Having declared that Quixote should embark on a new mission to bring sinners to repentance, he refers to the famous words spoken by Cervantes' hero on his death bed when he has renounced his former futile and insane quest to bring about the restoration of the age of chivalry. 'There are no birds this year in last year's nests' (24).[2] Though neither he nor Father Quixote understands the full meaning of the words, it is clear what Graham Greene is saying; that Father Quixote must put his past behind him just as Don Quixote has decided to disown his former quest, and concentrate on creating a new present and future.

The Bishop of Motopo has a secret plan for Quixote which he puts into effect. He informs the Pope of Father Quixote's kindness, whereupon the latter is elevated to the position of Monsignor, to the disgust and incomprehension of his own Bishop who, believing that Quixote is incapable of fulfilling his new role, arranges for him to have leave of absence. It also happens that the local Communist mayor, whose name, Zancas, is the original name of Cervantes' Sancho Panza, Don Quixote's servant, and who has thus acquired the name, Sancho, has failed to be re-elected as mayor and also has time to spare for a holiday. Thus Graham Greene, in emulating the original relationship between Cervantes' maverick hero and his servant, has created the basic framework of his story, a journey of the priest and the ex-mayor in the priest's car, Rocinante, with the relationship and dialogues between the humble, if maverick priest on furlough and the atheist, Communist ex-mayor. This becomes the basis for a series of amusing adventures and dialogues on political, social and religious matters, such as we have not witnessed previously in Greene's work and only comes to the fore in this, his late novel.

One critic has emphasized the importance in Greene's mind of making his priest sympathetic to a largely Protestant readership and has referred in some detail to the important antecedents of Greene's novel in order to demonstrate that the new relationship between the two travellers is in fact nothing new.[3] At the time of writing, in the early 1980s, most readers will have known of the Don Camillo stories by Giovanni Guareschi, where the relationship between the Communist mayor, Peppone, and the local priest, Don Camillo, is largely portrayed as very acrimonious, but where there turns out to be a strong degree of secret sympathy between the two men and the causes they espouse, demonstrated, among other instances, in the final scene of *The Little World of Don Camillo* when a gentle mood of Christmas goodwill is reached between the two antagonists. Greene has also in his novel *The Power and the Glory* shown us a priest who, despite being an alcoholic and fathering a child out of wedlock, sets an example in self-sacrificially returning to the danger zone and accepting the fate of his fellow priests. Such is the open honesty, kindness, sincerity and questioning mind of Father Quixote that he is from the start able to appeal to the individualistic Protestant spirit of Protestant readers as well as the sympathetic questioners among the Roman Catholics. We know also that he has never been 'troubled by sexual desires', as he says following his visit to the film *A Maiden's Prayer* (141), and as for his housekeeper, Teresa, she is described as being very unlikely to arouse sexual desire, being 'a square woman with protruding teeth and an embryo moustache' (15). There is therefore little likelihood that the prejudices of outsiders concerning the Catholic priesthood will be fulfilled. Father Quixote is in fact a totally likeable character and completely acceptable to humanity in general.

It is the purpose of this study to examine the extent of Father Quixote's questioning spirit, brought out so ingeniously and humorously through his interaction with the ex-mayor and his orthodox fellow Catholics, and while admitting the presence of his unorthodoxy, to demonstrate that in the final analysis, his instinctive Catholicism wins the day and 'last year's nests' can contain 'this year's birds' and the birds of the future.

Father Quixote and the Mayor, Sancho

Father Quixote is a mixture of conflicting responses to his priestly role. While we hear almost immediately of his sceptical view of the effectiveness of prayer and that 'so many of his prayers had remained unanswered' (11), we also register his words to his housekeeper when he states the importance of his mission to bring the Faith to unbelievers: 'If there were no heretics, Teresa, there would be little for a priest to do' (26). He owns a copy of a book of Moral Theology, a subject on which his replacement priest, the smug and pedantic Father Herrera, whose book on the subject is the old one written by Father Heribert Jone, is very knowledgeable and from which he quotes frequently. Father Quixote, however, much prefers the more devotional writings of St John of the Cross, St Teresa and St Francis de Sales, as well as the Gospels. At a key moment in the very strained conversation with Father Herrera, Greene has Father Quixote utter his guiding principle throughout his pastoral care of his people when he says that, apart from Moral Theology 'another sound base is God's love' (41), thus indicating the greater importance of basic principles of Christian love and service to others over dogma and theological reasoning. Yet, in one of his many dialogues with the ex-mayor, virtually all of which are concluded on a note of harmony over a bottle or several bottles of good wine, he is able to propound a convincing definition of the Trinity through his illustration of the three bottles of wine which they had drunk and which all contain the same wine even if there are three separate bottles. However, he is left feeling acute guilt over the fact that he had, in his own eyes, minimised the Holy Spirit by confining the Spirit to a mere half bottle! (52-53).

His emphasis on the love of God as demonstrated in practical ministry to the needs of people is shown in a way that also illustrates Greene's scepticism over aspects of religious procedure, ceremony and doctrine. While the question of contraception (81-85) is treated jokingly, the institution of confession is shown in a serious and critical light, as Father Quixote, when hearing the confession of a man who seeks him out, is worried that he may have failed him: 'He thought: I didn't say the right words. Why do I never find the right words? The man needed help and I recited a formula' (134). On the questions of hell and purgatory, Sancho claims that purgatory has been devised by the Church as a convenient escape from hell and that while Father Quixote may be uncomfortable with the concept of hell, it is found in the Bible. The priest admits that in St Matthew's Gospel the word occurs fifteen times. However, he is reassured by the fact that in St John the word 'hell' does not occur at all. Father Quixote feels that the concept of 'hell' is negating the principle of Love which he holds to above all, a point which he establishes early in his conversation with Father Herrera (57-58) and is crucial to our understanding of Greene's purpose in this novel.

Father Quixote's unhappiness with the idea of hell leads him defensively to challenge Sancho whether he had ever had any doubts about his Communist beliefs. While Sancho claims 'I try not to doubt' (58), the way has now been cleared for the two to air their different views on the importance of Belief and Doubt in their respective credos, and these issues become increasingly prominent in their discussions. Just as non-believers often find it relatively easy to confuse believers in their arguments, Father Quixote, who is more easily shaken in matters doctrinal than his more clever interlocutor (who after all had been a student at Salamanca University) is left wondering at the validity of many of the details that he has previously taken for granted, while holding fast to the principle of Love. In confirmation of this conviction that he had previously made in his conversation with Father Herrera, Quixote refers to the very long book by St Francis de Sales, *The Love of God,* and he adds: 'The word love doesn't come into Father Jone's rules and I think, perhaps I am wrong, that you won't find the phrase "mortal sin" in St Francis' book' (91). His instinct is against punitive concepts such as 'mortal sin'. He also admits a little earlier that his belief in hell is 'from obedience, not from the heart' (75). His kindly disposition revolts instinctively against such a concept, but he knows that belief in 'hell' and 'mortal sin' are tenets of the Faith.

At this point in their deliberations, while Father Quixote is feeling drowsy, he dozes off and has a dream. He dreams that the Crucifixion never took place, that 'Christ had been saved from the Cross by the legion of angels to which on an earlier occasion the Devil had told Him that he could appeal. So there was no final agony, no heavy stone which had to be rolled away, no discovery of an empty tomb.' In his dream Father Quixote saw Christ stepping down from the Cross 'triumphant and acclaimed'. Everyone, including the Roman soldiers, acclaim him. The disciples crowd round him and 'His mother smiled through her tears of joy. There was no ambiguity, no room for doubt and no room for faith at all. The whole world knew with certainty that Christ was the Son of God' (76-77).

Doubt and Faith

When Quixote awakes from his dream, he is filled with despair that in his dream his faith is a non-faith and that he has taken up a profession which is of use to no one, who must continue to live in a kind of

Saharan desert without doubt or faith, where everyone is certain that the same belief is true. He has found himself whispering: 'God save me from such a belief' (77). What is also interesting is the affinity he feels at that moment with the ex-mayor sleeping beside him on whose behalf Quixote mentally forms a prayer: 'Save him too from belief'. Perhaps he wants Sancho to stay as he is, a person with whom he can argue and dispute so that his own beliefs do not become stultified and anodyne. It is good to be able to argue with someone with whom one gets on well, especially when each has respect for the other's humanity and sense of justice, and when the dispute can finish amicably with a bottle of good wine! Despite their differences, Sancho is able a little later to comment to the Guardia that Monsignor Quixote 'has the kind of humility which is often to be found in holy men', both a compliment to Quixote and an ironical comment on the clergy (94).

Father Quixote thrives on the questions that fill his mind and that have left him throughout his life as a priest with the certainty that, despite his questions, he at least has his definite duty towards those who need him and need God's love. After his dream, in a subsequent conversation with Sancho on Communism, the Church and human rights, Quixote confirms what Sancho had earlier said, that he tries not to doubt (58) by saying that Sancho, in asserting that Russia, while only part way along the road to Communism, has nonetheless advanced further along the road than other countries, is demonstrating great faith in the future. But when the final perfect Communist state has arrived, Sancho's great-great-grandson, if he were of the same mind as Sancho, would have nothing more to believe in. Quixote asks: 'Can a man live without faith?' (80). A little later, he returns to the thought that flashed up in his dream: 'He would be living in a desert without end. No doubt. No faith.' Such a future would be arid. With reference to Sancho's 'great-great-grandson' the exchange continues as follows, with Quixote speaking first:

'I would prefer him to have what we call a happy
death.'
'What do you mean by a happy death?'
'I mean the hope of something further.'
'The beatific vision and all that nonsense? Believing in
some life eternal?'
'No. Not necessarily believing. We can't always believe.
Just having faith. Like you have, Sancho. Oh Sancho,
Sancho, it's an awful thing not to have doubts' (81).

Quixote distinguishes between faith and belief. Belief seems to apply
to an adherence to a system of assertions, such as a political credo. This
is undoubtedly what Sancho has. Quixote has no such certainties, but
thrives on the knife-edge position of living in a state of doubting
systems, while, despite his dream in which Christ does not suffer and
is not crucified, he holds fast to what he knows instinctively – that
there is no easy way without suffering, hardship, ambiguity, as he
thinks, 'no room for doubt and no room for faith at all' (77). A pre-
echo of this need for doubt is to be found in Miguel de Unamuno's
interpretation of Cervantes' novel, *Life of Don Quixote and Sancho*, in
which he attributes the following words to his hero: 'When most we
feel our separation from God, we are nearest to Him; and when we
least succeed in defining and picturing Him, we understand and love
Him most.'[4]

Quixote's airing of the necessity for doubt finds an echo in
Sancho's experience a little later when they arrive in Salamanca, where
for two years Sancho had listened to the distinguished theologian and
philosopher, Unamuno. Sancho tells his friend that in those days he
still had 'a half-belief' (110) and reminds Quixote that Unamuno was
very interested in Quixote's illustrious ancestor and studied Cervantes'
great novel. Unamuno's *Life of Don Quixote and Sancho* interprets the
course of events in the novel, but at this point the mayor refers to
Unamuno's important philosophical work *The Tragic Sense of Life*, in
which his own 'half-belief' finds a definite echo. Through the words of

Unamuno which considerably influenced Greene in his preparation of his novel and which the mayor refers to, we learn more of this vital theme of our study which is now taken to a higher level. This is prefaced by further consideration of an exchange between Quixote and Sancho and other concepts from Greene's work.

In his earlier novel, *The Human Factor,* Maurice Castle says of himself 'Perhaps I was born to be a half-believer',[5] and he describes Christ as 'that legendary figure whom he would have liked to believe in'.[6] Sancho's state of uncertainty at that time is echoed in the following exchange with Father Quixote who takes up the theme of Sancho's firm belief in communism now:

> 'And you have complete belief, don't you? In the
> prophet Marx. You don't have to think for yourself any
> more. Isaiah has spoken. You are in the hands of future
> history. How happy you must be with your complete
> belief. There's only one thing you will ever lack – the
> dignity of despair.' 'Have I complete belief?' Sancho
> asked. 'Sometimes I wonder. The ghost of my professor
> haunts me [...] I hear him saying, "There is a muffled
> voice, a voice of uncertainty which whispers in the ears
> of the believer. Who knows? Without this uncertainty
> how could we live?" '(112).[7]

Not only did Unamuno say these words in the lecture that Sancho heard, but he wrote them in his work, exactly as Sancho quotes them, words which Unamuno prefaces with several key thoughts at this crucial stage in the section of his work entitled 'In the Depths of the Abyss'. He writes:

> Shall we doubt that we think, that we feel, that we are?
> Nature does not allow it; she forces us to believe even
> when our reason is not convinced! Absolute certainty
> and absolute doubt are both alike forbidden to us. We
> hover in a vague mean between these two extremes,
> as between being and nothingness; for complete

scepticism would be the extinction of the intelligence
and the total death of man. But it is not given to man
to annihilate himself; there is in him something which
invincibly resists destruction, I know not what vital
faith, indomitable even by his will. Whether he likes it
or not, he must believe, because he must act, he must
preserve himself. His reason, if he listened only to that,
would reduce him to a state of absolute inaction; he
would perish even before he had been able to prove to
himself that he existed.[8]

Man cannot rely on reason for certainty, yet complete doubt would destroy him. He continues: 'Scepticism is produced by the clash between reason and desire. And from this clash, from this embrace between despair and scepticism, is born that holy, that sweet, that saving incertitude, which is our complete consolation.'[9]

Shortly afterwards, Unamuno quotes from the words of the man who came to Jesus: 'Lord, I believe; help thou mine unbelief.'[10] Just as Maurice Castle wants to believe in Christ, but is unable to, the believer seeks certainty, but also seeks the supreme consolation of doubt which at least keeps him searching and restless for the truth. Many claim that they are anxious because of their uncertainty and feel that faith means absolute certainty. In a recent television programme, the Chief Rabbi, interviewed by four well-known atheists, defined faith as 'the courage to embrace uncertainty'.[11]

Total certainty, the product of reason, leads in Unamuno's view to stultification of the will to act and the death of the spirit. But Sancho has embraced the certainty of belief in his developing Communist revolution. However, that does not prevent him from drawing closer to Father Quixote in a growing friendship arising out of their honest differences, their love of justice and Sancho's knowledge of Quixote's love of suffering humanity evinced in his donation to *In Vinculis*.

It is becoming clear that the differences in the attitudes of the two men are decreasing. Sancho also has a dream in which he is searching for Father Quixote who is lost and whom he eventually finds in a church where he is perched high up on the altar 'like a sacred image' and is being mocked by the congregation, a foretaste of events to come (164). He is sympathetic towards his companion in his suffering, even though he still cannot accept his opinions.

Gradually, as they drink increasing quantities of wine which have of course lubricated their discussions and created many of the risqué views that have been expressed, they fall increasingly foul of the police, and Father Quixote is captured and brought back home by his Bishop in a state of unconsciousness. He is deemed to be insane, like his great ancestor, but he manages to escape with the help of Teresa and Sancho and they take to the road again, endeavouring to evade the police's interest in Rocinante which has been re-sprayed.

Quixote Renewed

This second part of the story reveals a Father Quixote who is much more resolute in the course of action he wants to take. He has been forbidden to conduct mass, and, when his Bishop accuses Sancho in his absence of leading Father Quixote astray into dangerous Communist views, Father Quixote counters him decisively: 'It wasn't that he *led* me, Excellency. He gave me the opportunity [...] on this holiday I have felt a freedom' (190). This is the first time that the word 'freedom' has occurred in the story, and it marks the beginning of a new approach on the part of Father Quixote to events from now on.

His attitude to faith has indeed changed, though now he talks of 'belief' whereas previously he associated 'belief' with political systems. As he departs with Sancho, he thinks: 'how is it that when I speak of belief, I become aware always of a shadow, the shadow of disbelief haunting my belief?' (197). He has always been prone to doubts and has indeed thrived on them, but he now seems to have developed a definite antipathy towards all systems and wants to act with total independence of spirit, simply following the leading of God, saying that it was through God's leading that they had progressed previously. 'Do we have to make plans, Sancho? Last time we went a bit here and a bit there, at random. You won't agree, of course, but in a way we left ourselves in the hands of God.' When he then says that 'God moves very mysteriously – perhaps He wanted me to meet the bishop' (197), it almost seems as if he is answering his feeling, expressed at the opening of the story, that 'so many of his prayers had remained unanswered' (11). When, in answer to Sancho's question whether they should head towards the Basques or the Galicians, he suggests: 'Let's leave the details to God' (198), a thought very different from the feeling that he expresses at the very start of their journey when he speaks of his apprehension at leaving home: 'We have just left La Mancha and nothing seems safe any more' (44). Through his experiences, he has matured into an understanding that he can indeed feel safe in the hands of God. But his new boldness makes him careless at the first opportunity of action, and he takes on the manner of his ancestor in attempting to right the wrongs that he sees. At this stage in the story, Quixote begins to tilt at windmills like his ancestor and has to witness the disastrous results as his ancestor did.[12]

They are now realising increasingly that they have very much more in common than they had once thought. Both seem to have fallen foul of the institutions they represent. They describe themselves as 'survivors' who have more belief in the basic credos of their systems than in the systems themselves. Quixote tells Sancho that he seems 'to have more belief in Communism than in the Party' while Sancho reiterates with the corresponding thought that his companion has 'more belief in Catholicism than in Rome'. Add then the exchange:

> 'Belief? Oh, belief. Perhaps you are right, Sancho. But
> perhaps it's not belief that really matters.'
> 'What do you mean, father? I thought...'

'Did the Don really believe in Amadis of Gaul, Roland
and all his heroes – or was it only that he believed in
the virtues they stood for?' (204).

Father Quixote has come to the conclusion that the belief is less important than the underlying moral code that guides our behaviour. When he confirms to his companion that he is 'riddled by doubts' and 'sure of nothing, not even of the existence of God' but that 'doubt is human' and that he wants 'to believe that it is all true' (205), which is his only certainty, he seems to be going much further than previously, even though he has always doubted.

In a previous conversation when the two arrive in Salamanca and Sancho describes the uncertainties that he felt on hearing the words of Unamuno, he had countered the point that his companion has just made, that with his firm beliefs in his cause he will never lack 'the dignity of despair' (112). Graham Greene's earlier priest in *The Power and the Glory* describes despair as 'the unforgivable sin',[13] and earlier in that novel Father José had felt the same despair, also described as 'the unforgivable sin'[14] but now, in Father Quixote's eyes, despair has a much more positive meaning, regardless of the fact that it is an extreme expression of doubt. Father Quixote, in contrast to Father José, has throughout given a much more positive account of himself with his kindly humanity, thus enabling him to present 'despair' in a dignified light, whereas Father José had up to that point in the story been seen in a much more negative light. Even if Father Quixote has on occasion allowed his doubts to sink into a dignified despair, he is from now on in the story going to demonstrate that positive action to right wrongs is following the will of God and is the antidote to both doubt and despair, the latter no longer seen in a theologically negative light.

A code of righting wrongs brings him very much into line with his companion who is also against injustice in society. But we are soon to see that Father Quixote is more intent on pursuing his convictions than Sancho who sees the risks and wants to err on the side of caution. From now on Father Quixote becomes the initiator, even if he makes errors of judgement, and Sancho becomes the timid and cautious one. Bernard Bergonzi makes the point that, when Quixote's bishop describes the priest as suffering from a mental breakdown, it certainly looks as if at this point in the story he has been proved right.[15] The priest steps into the role of his illustrious ancestor, challenging the first wrong that he sees, regardless of the danger. This challenge comes on arrival in Galicia, on the way to a Trappist monastery where they hope to find sanctuary until the police search is over.

When they arrive in Galicia, they hear of malpractice among a company of priests who are selling pardons to those donating money to the church and thus desecrating the image of the Virgin Mary who in the procession is clothed in paper and receiving the donations. Father Quixote is outraged and in his fury resolves to do as his ancestor would have done, attack the priests and disperse the procession. The priest, Señor Diego, who has informed him of this abuse, advises him: 'Go and see for yourself' and Quixote sees this as his duty: 'You have told me my duty. "Go and see for yourself" ' (223). He is echoing the response of Greene's earlier priest who, despite his human weaknesses, acts from a sense of duty in not running away from his people and later in responding to the bogus call of the treacherous half-caste who has called on him to give the last rights to a dying American bandit.[16] And of course, Father Quixote himself had earlier responded, though reluctantly, to the needs of the man seeking to confess (134).

However, while Cervantes' hero embarks on the imaginary crusade against the windmills, believing them to be giants, Father Quixote, having donned his 'armour', his purple *perchera* and his collar, sets out to defy the procession as a real abuse, denouncing it as blasphemy. As he does so, his instinctive love of the Madonna rises up in him, as he 'gazed up at the crowned head and the glassy eyes which were like those of a woman dead and neglected – no one had bothered even to lower her lids. He thought: was it for this she saw her son die in agony? To collect money? To make a priest rich?'. When he is told that this is their feast day and that it has the blessing of their bishop, he protests at their treatment of Our Lady. 'Put down Our Lady [...] How dare you [...] clothe her like that in money?' (227). The Guardia are called, the procession is disrupted and Monsignor Quixote is denounced as an impostor. As their car, Rocinante, leaves for the monastery of Osera, they are chased by the Guardia, whereupon on their arrival there is an accident and a concussed, seriously injured Quixote is carried into the monastery.

He is comatose after his concussion, but in his delirium at the monastery he celebrates a doctrinally dubious Mass without the elements. Murray Roston reminds us that in *The Power and the Glory* the priest 'continued to offer communion even after the altar stone had been lost, representing Greene's suggestion that, in extreme circumstances, the technical requirements of ritual are less important than the intent of the celebrant'. Roston then points out that, though Quixote had been debarred from celebrating mass, 'the antipathy aroused by the bishop responsible for the debarment reduces the disqualification to a merely doctrinal and hence nugatory factor', which, one might add, would put Quixote in a favourable light with Catholics who understand the spirit of his act, performed instinctively in his delirium.[17] There is an outsider present, a visiting professor of Hispanic studies, a nominal Catholic and a rationalist, who does not recognise the validity of Father Quixote's actions. Thus, the contrast between his rationalism and Quixote's instinctive celebration of his unorthodox mass puts rationalism in an unfavourable light and strengthens our admiration for the priest.

As Quixote lies in bed, he seems to assume the role of his ancestor who offers his servant Sancho a governorship which Sancho accepts and fulfils effectively, but soon relinquishes. However, Father Quixote does not offer him a governorship, but a kingdom. 'Come with me, and you will find the kingdom,' he says (246). A Christian would, of course, grasp the connection with the Kingdom of God, but this is lost on Sancho who simply says that he will never leave the one with whom he has already come so far and for so long. When Father Quixote gets up from his bed and moves towards the stairs, they allow him to act out his dream and he starts to conduct Mass, something that we have not seen during the course of the story, but which fulfils his role as priest. It is interesting that, apart from the Our Father, he remembers the *Agnus Dei*, whose words *qui tollis peccata mundi* (249) are in marked contrast to his earlier dream in which he rejects the idea of a suffering, crucified Christ (76-77). He is definitely returning to the fundamental tenets of the faith that he has served. In recalling the words of the *Agnus Dei* he also whispers 'Lamb of God, but the goats, the goats', recalling previous words of his from the bed in which he had been laid, when he says: 'Excellency, a lamb may be able to tame an elephant, but I would beg you to remember the goats in your prayers' (245). This in turn recalls his conversation with Sancho in which the latter propounds his own version of the meaning of Christ's word to Peter on the shore of the lake following his resurrection 'Feed my sheep' (55),[18] which he then follows with a query why sheep are preferred to goats who have all the same qualities. In fact, he says, the goat gives his skin in man's service while the sheep only gives his wool (56). Quixote is left wondering and feeling that goats have been neglected as the object of Christian service. As Quixote now recalls these allusions, he is making it clear in his delirium that it is the weak, the needy, the neglected who are largely in his thoughts.

As Quixote approaches the altar, he offers the Mass to Sancho, albeit without the wafer or the wine. As he holds out his hand to Sancho he addresses him as 'compañero', asking him to kneel, whereupon Sancho repeats the word in his turn (250). Quixote then collapses and dies.

A discussion follows whether the phantom Mass is valid or not. The visiting professor denies its validity, saying there is no bread and wine, but then the priest in charge, Father Leopoldo, counters him: 'I know as well as you – or as little – yes, I agree to that. But Monsignor Quixote quite obviously believed in the presence of the bread and wine. Which of us was right?' (253). When the professor continues to deny its validity, Father Leopoldo asks him: 'Do you think it's more difficult to turn empty air into wine than wine into blood? Can our limited senses decide a thing like that? We are faced by an infinite mystery' (254).[19]

He is surely saying that, as the Mass is such a mystery when one considers the transformation of wine into blood, if the intention is present when no wine or bread are available, then the Eucharist is valid. What is also important, however, is that Sancho is reached with the missing elements and takes them, though he still denies any faith and still claims to be a Communist. But Father Leopoldo reminds him that he and Monsignor Quixote had drawn together in friendship. Ultimately, Sancho is left thinking about the meaning of love that has conquered hate and whether this love for Quixote will last:

> Why is it that the hate of man – even of a man like
> Franco – dies with his death, and yet love, the love
> which he had begun to feel for Father Quixote, seemed
> now to live and grow in spite of the final separation
> and the final silence – for how long, he wondered with
> a kind of fear, was it possible for that love of his to
> continue? And to what end? (256).

So has Father Quixote died as a madman whereas his famous ancestor died in an enlightened state, regretting his delusions and accepting that 'there are no birds this year in last year's nests' (24), that it is futile to rely on the achievements of the past in the expectation that he will find renewal this year? Before he had set out on his journey with the ex-mayor he had had a dream in which he had climbed a high tree and dislodged an empty nest, dry and brittle, 'a relic of a year gone by' (37), confirming his awareness that he must start again and find new pastures. And yet, as the story has developed after his initial apprehension at embarking on a journey into the unknown, a definite change has taken place, suggesting both a leap into new ways and a newly found trust in the old.

Conclusion

What, then, has taken place? The man who has been plagued by doubts and uncertainties about his role and the church he has represented, has always believed in the supreme importance of God's love and his own love as a priest for those who need him. But he has had to learn that he would not advance in his vision of life until he had set out on this journey, even though the journey frightened him, as Sancho says: 'It wasn't until he left his village that your ancestor encountered the windmills' (96). After his enforced return home and his escape, the change is most marked. Formerly he had disputed with Sancho who seemed to leave Father Quixote with doubts about his own feelings, but now he seems to be prepared to launch out into new ventures, trusting God's will and guidance, regardless of the consequences. It is now Sancho who has become more cautious and hesitant.

Father Quixote, in launching out again, has rediscovered what are some of the fundamentals of his faith. He has discovered that he loves the Virgin Mary and hates any blasphemous defilement of her image. He has discovered his sense of duty in protecting her or at least endeavouring to do so, in the spirit of his ancestor, though Father Quixote's cause is not an imaginary one. We know that he had already adhered to duty in hearing the confession of the man who sought his help and in absolving him, though he senses that he has pronounced mere words, a formula. Now his sense of duty is no longer a reluctant one, but one that compels him forward. He has discovered throughout his journey that there is more common

182

ground between him and the ex-mayor than he had ever thought despite their friendship, a point that he confirms when he tells his companion: 'You are my moral theologian, Sancho' (163). On this basis he seals this in his offering of the invisible wafer and wine to his unbelieving friend. Perhaps this is the fulfilment of his early words to his housekeeper, Teresa, when he jokingly says: 'If there were no heretics, Teresa, there would be little for a priest to do' (26).

This brings us to the final rediscovery that Father Quixote has made – that his instinct takes him back to the Mass, that even if the visible elements are missing, he can in spirit celebrate the Mass and realise the invisible presence of the body and blood of the Christ who has suffered and borne the sins of the world. Again this conviction had not deserted him, as witnessed in his dream and in his defiant statement to Sancho when he says that, despite all his cynical companion's findings from reading Quixote's books, he holds to the 'historic fact. That Christ died on the Cross and rose again' (85). His convictions had become confused by moments of low self-esteem, sense of failure and doubts reinforced by friendly arguments with his more intelligent travelling companion. Like all Christians suffering acute doubts, even in the worst of times, he had held to the historic tenets of his beliefs. So Monsignor Quixote has returned to the essence of his priestly convictions, duties and commitments. Though he does not live to continue his rediscovery, he has surely found that 'this year's birds' and indeed last year's can continue to live in 'last year's nests'.

This article was first published in *The Heythrop Journal,* November 2013.

Endnotes

1   Graham Greene, *Monsignor Quixote* (first published in 1982, this edition published by Vintage, 2000), 23. All future references to the novel are given in brackets in the text.

2   Cervantes' words are as spoken in Greene's text by the Bishop. Miguel de Cervantes' original words in his epic 1605 novel, *Don Quixote,* translated by Walter Starkie (Macmillan 1957 and Signet Classic, New American Library 1964), 1048, are in Starkie's translation: 'One should never look for birds of this year in the nests of yesteryear.' Starkie's translation, in my view, has much more of a period flavour.

3   Murray Roston, *Graham Greene's Narrative Strategies* (Palgrave Macmillan 2006), 141ff.

4   Miguel de Unamuno, *Life of Don Quixote and Sancho,* translated by A.A. Knopf, 1927), 236.

5   Graham Greene, *The Human Factor* (The Bodley Head, 1978), 135.

6   Greene, *Human Factor*, 187.

7   Miguel de Unamuno, *The Tragic Sense of Life,* translated by J.E. Crawford, first published by Macmillan 1921, this edition Fontana 1962, 126.

8   Unamuno, *Tragic Sense,* 125.

9   Unamuno, *Tragic Sense,* 126.

10 Unamuno, *Tragic Sense* 127. The biblical reference is to Mk 9.24.

11 Jonathan Sacks, BBC1, 6 September 2010.

12 Miguel de Cervantes, *Don Quixote,* chapter VIII, 98-99. See note 2.

13 Graham Greene, *The Power and the Glory* (Heinemann and the Bodley Head, 1971), 68.

14 Greene, *Power and Glory*, 54.

15 Bernard Bergonzi, *A Study in Greene* (Oxford University Press 2006), 181.

16 Greene, *Power and Glory,* 74 and 213ff. respectively.

17 Roston, *Narrative Structures,* 154.

18 The biblical reference is to Jn 21.18.

19 This most sympathetic of priests, Father Leopoldo, is surely named after Graham Greene's friend, Father Duran, Leopoldo, who writes in his book, *Graham Greene: Friend and Brother* (Fount Paperbacks 1995) that Greene described his novel to him at the outset as 'a book that will never be finished'. But the presence of the fictional Leopoldo at the death of Father Quixote is surely confirmation of Duran's answer to Greene: 'Of course, you'll finish this book. You must!' (213).

Become as a Little Child
Reflections on Georges Bernanos' *Diary of a Country Priest* and other works

Children

In a letter to a Brazilian girl in 1939 during his stay in Brazil, Georges Bernanos writes: 'Be faithful to poets, remain faithful to childhood. Never become an adult.'[1] But in his novel *Monsieur Ouine*, which Bernanos completed in 1941 after ten years of stop-start work on the novel, he places the words 'I have always honoured childhood. Childhood is the salt of the earth. Let it lose its taste, and the world will soon become nothing but rot and gangrene'[2] in the mouth of the eponymous main character who shows through the course of the novel, despite his many good words, that he is a corrupting influence on children and on the entire village of Fenouille.

The purpose of this study is to examine the duality in the mind and writings of the French Catholic novelist and polemicist, Georges Bernanos (1888-1948), who sees the wonder and glory of childhood as well as its vulnerability and fragility. In his works, children are both victims and yet vehicles of grace and beauty. Before focusing on his most celebrated novel, *Diary of a Country Priest*, it is important to consider in his earlier works the position of children and of similar, pure spirits who in his eyes have many of the characteristics of children.

In *Sous le soleil de Satan*, Bernanos' first novel written in 1926 when he is still troubled by his memories of the First World War and sees the world as a vast struggle between good and evil, the young priest, Father Donissan, himself has many of the characteristics of a child, in his apparent naivety and innocence, his impulsiveness and gaucheness. His father confessor sees him as 'a child, a real child',[3] but he has the gift of insight into the motives of those he meets and serves. In his priesthood in this parish he is confronted with the fate of Mouchette, a young girl who has been seduced by the local lord of the manor whom she then kills. When he meets her, Father Donissan, despite her spirit of revolt against him, tells her: 'I have seen the name of God written on your heart',[4] and later tells her: 'You believe you have killed a man. Poor girl! You have freed yourself from him.'[5] That is true, as the man she had killed had been oppressing her, but, in her despair, she cuts her throat. Donissan, who tried to save her soul by carrying her to church, is unable to save her life. He is rebuked by his superior: 'You have acted like a child.'[6] But Donissan has other strengths, which will be considered shortly.

In a subsequent novel, *La joie*, we find a young girl, Chantal, who has all the qualities of a saint. In the novel immediately preceding it, *L'imposture*, which acts as the first part of the two novels taken together, she has been influenced by a saintly priest, Father Chevance, described in the novel as a 'child's soul'.[7] We only see her fully in the sequel, *La joie*. The novel contains frequent references to her as a child, in one of which her nature is described as 'pure', like 'water so pure',[8] at another showing 'unyielding purity'.[9] She herself speaks of her humble dependence on God's will for her: 'I would like to be nothing but a little grain of intangible dust held suspended in God's will.'[10] However, she is firmly earthbound, freely accepting her role of running her father's household, including the Russian chauffeur who lusts after her and finally kills her. Her purity remains unsullied, but she is very vulnerable, like Mouchette in Bernanos' first novel. In *Monsieur Ouine*, the picture of childhood is different. Monsieur

Ouine, a retired teacher of languages, observes the parish of Fenouille with a sardonic, lustful eye. At school, he had been corrupted and sexually abused by his history teacher, and Ouine describes himself in his final conversation with the boy, Steeny, as consumed by curiosity: 'I am devoured by curiosity [...] I have only been hungry for souls.'[11] He has corrupted Steeny, who visits him in his room, is plied with madeira and finds himself both drawn to and yet repulsed by the presence of Monsieur Ouine. Contrasted with the example of the good, if naïve priest, Father Donissan, in *Sous le soleil de Satan*, Ouine is described by Gerda Blumenthal as 'the false priest of Fenouille [...] a counterfeit figure of love and innocence'. She continues: 'His sexual ambiguity [...] suggests childlike innocence. His unctuous manner suggests the priest.'[12] It is almost a fulfilment of the statement made by Mouchette's father in *Sous le soleil de Satan*: 'Priests pervert the conscience of children',[13] which might be considered an unconscious foretaste of what is to come in Bernanos' writings.

Bernanos seems to be so interested in the character of Mouchette that he uses her name again in an entirely different short novel, *Nouvelle histoire de Mouchette,* in which his child character, living in dire circumstances in a broken home, is raped and in despair drowns herself. Like many of Bernanos' child characters, she was born and lived in poverty, which is another of the features of childhood in his work. Father Donissan, too, and the priest of Fenouille in *Monsieur Ouine* also endure poverty in childhood, as does the eponymous priest in *Diary of a Country Priest*, which will be considered in detail later.

Priests and Church

Not only are children at the very centre of the struggle between good and evil, representing both innocence and vulnerability. As we are seeing, priests too become the battleground where the war between good and evil is waged. In *Sous le soleil de Satan*, the childlike priest who has such insight into the needs and problems of those he encounters is graphically assailed by a Satan figure whom he manages to repel, but who continues to launch a spiritual assault on his soul, just as Christ, assailed in the wilderness, manages to defeat the devil who, according to Luke, leaves him 'until an opportune time' (Lk. 4.13). Donissan is destined not to experience peace in his heart. 'This priest is appointed to dispense to others the peace that he will never know' is the author's comment.[14] Bernanos, still dominated by his memories of the Great War, is acutely aware of the power of evil, and for the priest, the central representative of God in the parish, the pressure of temptation to surrender to the assaults of the devil is so great that he is only just able to win the victory. He is deemed by a fellow priest to be a saint, but Donissan does not see his saintliness as a victory. 'The man of the Cross is not there to conquer, but to testify unto death of the fierce cunning, the unjust and vile power, the iniquitous judgement with which he (Satan) appeals to God.'[15] His faith comes at a price, the price of his own peace of mind. His last words are: 'You wanted my peace [...] come and take it!'[16]

In *L'imposture*, the worldly, cynical priest, Father Cénabre, has lost his faith and settles for arid, cerebral scholarship. He is able 'to write about holiness, as if charity didn't exist'.[17] He is an example of what Bernanos criticises so strongly in the life of the church, its formalism, its order without the fire of the Spirit. In his polemical work, *Les grands cimetières sous la lune*, written in 1937, he expresses powerful criticism of the failings of the Church, which he sees as betraying the Incarnation of Christ in a 'disincarnation of the Word'.[18] The term 'disincarnation' is a term that Bernanos invents and may be seen as reflecting the emptiness and aridity of the words in Father Cénabre's cerebral, scholastic offerings and the shallow volubility of the ex-teacher of languages, Monsieur Ouine, who pours out empty words to those who come to see him, words that cajole and seduce, but are ultimately without meaning except to reflect the emptiness of his spirit. In *Les grands cimetières sous la lune*, Bernanos writes in explanation of his term 'disincarnation': 'Your faith is no longer alive, it has become abstract, it has, so to speak, lost its flesh.'[19] The British Catholic writer, Gerald Vann, echoes Bernanos' criticism of the Church less forcefully, but nonetheless relevantly: 'We must make sure that we are learning to see and love the law of God in terms of the life of God [...] Our Lord came primarily not to bring us an ethical code, but to bring us life.'[20] He is making the same point, that the life risks being drained from the western Church, and Bernanos maintains that 'Christendom has died, Europe is going to die'[21] and that true 'Christian faith dwells essentially in Christ'.[22] He has already stated this in his polemical work *La grande peur des bien-pensants* in which he claims that the living image of Christ has been degraded and that 'social Christians only speak his name, but are happy to applaud him'.[23] He claims that for the Church 'salvation is within your grasp. Do not try to go there by four different routes. There is only one, that of poverty.'[24]

The Church, he asserts, has become too preoccupied with status, formalism and legalism. In *Les grands cimetières sous la lune* he maintains that, in its formalism and estrangement from the spirit of Christ, the Church must recapture His spirit. The loss of the true spirit of the Church is mentioned again in *Diary of a Country Priest*, written in 1936, when the priest meets the young soldier, Olivier, whose criticisms of the Church are extremely cogent. Olivier claims that the nation has been secularised and that there is now only 'the pagan state'. He had just expressed the strong view that

> There are no more soldiers. No soldiers, no
> Christianity. You'll say the Church has survived and
> that's the chief thing [...] But Christ's Kingdom on
> earth will never be again [...] The last soldier died on
> 30 May 1431, and you killed her, you people. Not
> only killed her: condemned her, cut her off, burned
> her.[25]

The priest points out that the Church also made her, Joan of Arc, a saint (193). It is important that she was hardly more than a child and demonstrated total self-belief, total commitment, impulsiveness, saintliness and the innocence of childhood. To return to *Les grands cimetières sous la lune*, Bernanos, in his conviction of the supreme importance of childhood, issues his clarion call: 'Become like children again.' In this he refers to the spirit of St Thérèse of Lisieux (1873-1897) who 'preached the spirit of childhood'.[26] Bernanos had been reading the writings of St Thérèse at the time of writing *La joie* and the character of the heroine of that work, the saintly Chantal, testifies fully to this. The resemblance between Chantal and Saint Thérèse is contrasted with the subtle and cynical criticism of her by Father Cénabre in *L'imposture*, emphasising the distance he has travelled from a true, simple and innocent faith in Christ.[27] The scholar Michael R. Tobin draws attention to the point that, contrary to normal Catholic practice, there is no crucifix in Father Cénabre's room. What he sees is an empty cross reflecting an early obsession and loathing of the sight of the sufferings of Christ on the Cross which demonstrate the presence of love.[28] The attitude of Father Cénabre is in Bernanos' view a reflection of the aridity and impersonality of the official Church as a whole. But Father Cénabre ultimately comes under the influence of his association with Chantal at the end of *La joie* and is turned back towards true faith, but at the price of his sanity. Bernanos is convinced that the Church since the end of the Middle Ages needs the virtues of childhood innocence and enthusiasm to temper the apparent strength and maturity of its adult authorities. Gerald Vann again recaptures this just a few years after Bernanos is writing, when he writes that the Church needs 'to be zealous, to have the strength of will of the man, but also [...] to be filled [...] with the freshness and spontaneity, the zest and enthusiasm of the child'.[29]

Diary of a Country Priest

When we now come to consider in more detail Bernanos' most celebrated novel, *Diary of a Country Priest*, we find a very interesting comment by the author himself in the Introduction to *Les grands cimetières sous la lune*, where he comments on the fact that, of all the priests he describes, the priest of Ambricourt, the central character in *Diary of a Country Priest*, (hereafter referred to as Ambricourt) is the only one to whom he does not give a name, but whom he loves more than any other.[30] Malcolm Scott in his monograph on the novel asks the rhetorical question: 'Is it not significant that the curé himself has no name, except that of the parish, Ambricourt, to which he has given his entire essence? Does his namelessness not convey the integrity of his person and his one-ness with his flock?'[31] This might appear to contradict the impression the priest himself gains from his hostile parish, but Bernanos himself felt he could identify with him. This is the happiest of his novels, the one in which Bernanos finds the greatest fulfilment. Such is his relish of this new work, that he suspends work on *La paroisse morte* ('the dead parish') on which he has been engaged intermittently since 1931 and whose title he changes to *Monsieur Ouine*. Robert Speaight suggests a good reason for this decision. He suggests that in his work on *La paroisse morte*, Bernanos had reached chapter 16 where the young priest of Fenouille is in conversation with the mayor. He continues: 'Behind the young curé of Fenouille had arisen the figure of another curé who was to be the *curé de campagne*. Thus from the corrupted heart of the *paroisse morte* was conceived the masterpiece whose birth would not now be long delayed.'[32] His new novel, written in diary form and thus encapsulating more of his own intimate reflections and soul searchings, produces a high degree of spiritual satisfaction and becomes the high point of his statements on God and the Church. Malcolm Scott further makes the very important point that the first person narration of this novel has a special significance:

> In Catholic novels written in the traditional third-
> person form, the responsibility for conveying the
> novelist's religious perceptions is devolved to the
> narrator; thus presumptions of God's role in the affairs
> of human beings are written into the fabric of the

entire text, and for readers unable to accept them, the
novel as a whole risks rejection. In *Diary of a Country
Priest*, the experience of religious emotion – doubt,
despair, joy – is conveyed wholly from within the
central character, as a psychological strand within the
fiction.

Even though readers may reject the Catholic and spiritual basis of belief, the encounter with the psychological processes in the experience of the first-person narrator, in Scott's view, 'constitutes for most readers the accessibility and indeed universality of Bernanos' text'.[33] For this reason I believe that this novel represents the essence of Bernanos' personal convictions and is his most successful expression of them.

As in his previous works, the priest is the centre of attention, his soul the battleground in the war between good and evil. This is stated clearly in one of his meditations in the novel where it appears that the battle between good and evil seems to be an even contest: 'The world of sin confronts the world of grace.' He continues: 'There is not only a communion of saints, there is a communion of sinners' (108). In his parish 'good and evil are probably equally distributed, but on such a low plane' (1). While it is not dead, it is 'eaten up with boredom' (2), and he is aware that there is 'a cancerous growth within us' (1). This foretaste of the eventual revelation of Ambricourt's own cancer sets the scene for the drama that will be played out round the lives of the people in the château and in his own body and soul.

The young priest was born and grew up in poverty, and his body is tainted with the results of eating a diet of poor food throughout his childhood and youth, which he now continues with his daily diet including poor quality wine. He is so poor that he has to be fed with extra food and drink by his parishioners, and he is wrongly assumed by the community to be an alcoholic. It emerges gradually that he is seriously ill, not only with alcohol poisoning, and his spiritual musings are thus strongly influenced by his poor physical state which turns out to be due to stomach cancer. His musings are tending towards his death and could therefore be considered by some readers as rather unbalanced and morbid.

While he is himself naïve in his early dealings with the people of his parish, he soon finds that the children in his confirmation class show distinct strains of malice. One girl, Séraphita, ogles him and he is secretly mocked by the other children for supposed favouritism. The more important instance of childhood malice is found in the person of Chantal, the daughter of the count and countess: Chantal, the namesake of the saintly Chantal of his earlier novel, but in her malicious nature showing a totally different character, comes to play a key role in the development of the story. But in the choice of name for both children, Bernanos is again highlighting the dual tendencies of human nature towards both good and evil.

One of the key factors in the novel is the character of the curé of the neighbouring parish of Torcy, an older, much wiser priest from whom Ambricourt learns much and with whom he holds several important conversations. These often take the form of lengthy monologues in which Torcy (as we shall call him) conveys his wisdom and compensates for the limited wisdom and experience of Ambricourt, at least in the first half of the novel. While Monsieur Ouine in the other novel uses words to lead towards subterfuge and corruption, Torcy uses words at similar length to create the wisdom of saintliness, the antidote of light against the darkness of the other man. But Torcy is by no means unworldly: he has a strong awareness of the fact of evil in the world, expressed most powerfully at one point at the end of his monologue to the younger priest when, while expressing the hope of the redemption of humanity he says:

> But just you wait. Wait for the quarter-of-an-hour's
> silence. Then the Word will be heard of men – not the
> voice they rejected which spoke so quietly: "I am the
> Way, the Resurrection and the Life" – but the voice
> from the depths: "I am the door for ever locked, the

road which leads nowhere, the lie, the everlasting dark"
(16).

Despite the earthy realism and gaiety of much of his conversation, this demonstrates the acute sadness at the heart of this man and furthermore the sadness at the heart of the author, much of whose nature is expressed through the thoughts of Torcy as well as of Ambricourt. Speaight expresses this relationship as follows: 'He (Torcy) is the virile counterpart to the young curé's diffident sensitivity […] In their conversations it is as if one part of Bernanos were coming to the rescue of the other.'[34] One of the most poignant thoughts echoing this sadness comes later when Ambricourt says to a reformed Séraphita: 'I'm sad […] because God isn't loved enough' (180).

The central event in the story is the long conversation between the priest and the countess that occupies over twenty pages in the middle of the novel. The countess has said very little and appears only occasionally until that point. The priest has known for some time that the countess had a son who died in infancy eleven years previously. He has gone to see her to talk about her daughter, Chantal, who is accusing her father, the count, of having an affair with the governess, Madame Louise. He approaches the conversation with almost aggressive frankness, offending her by his tone, yet arriving at the truth and able to convict her in her spirit of faults that had remained buried deep in her soul since the death of her child. At one point, the priest, almost instinctively, makes a verbal stab in the dark: 'You don't love your daughter, Madame' (117). When she reacts angrily, the exchange continues with the priest speaking first:

> 'I'm not clever enough to have thought out anything
> beforehand. You yourself put those words into my
> mouth, and I'm very sorry they offend you.'
> 'I suppose you think you can read my heart.'
> 'Yes, Madame, I think I can' (118).

He has indeed shown that he has insight into the motives of those he is talking to, very much like the earlier priest, Donissan. A little later, he explains how he manages to gain such insight. 'For my daring can be explained: probably I had lost my nerve, gone blindly on burning my boats as shy people often do. To make quite certain of doing my duty.' In his musings he continues his explanation: 'For some time now I have had the impression that my mere presence will draw sin out [...] As though the enemy scorned to hide himself from such a puny adversary, as though he came to defy me openly, laugh in my face' (120).

She has been taken by surprise by his skill in counselling: 'You've a trick in drawing one out. You're a sly little priest!' (122). This leads her to confess the sorry story of her reactions to the death of her son and her family relationships ever since, her bitterness over the loss of her infant son and her daughter's consequent resentment and behaviour. As she starts to explain and the priest fears that her daughter, in her frustration and anguish, may be driven to extremes, she dismisses this as unlikely. When the priest then says that such people who appear to be afraid of death are the very ones who might be tempted to try it, he speaks in a manner unlike his previous self. The exchange is as follows, with the priest speaking first:

> 'Void fascinates those who daren't look into it. They
> throw themselves in, for fear of falling.'
> 'Who taught you that? You must have seen it
> somewhere in a book. It can't be simply your own
> experience' (123).

Again one could argue that the priest is speaking out of character, that his words are unrealistic. But as she says, he seems to have the gift of acute insight, of drawing out the truth. But he is also speaking in the manner of a poet, with the author Bernanos speaking imaginatively and instinctively both as priest and poet to arrive at the truth. It seems to be a pre-echo of what he will say later to the Brazilian girl that was mentioned above, namely that as a priest with such direct insight he is recapturing the instincts of childhood which he equates with the imagination of the poet.[35]

Again we notice a contrast with Monsieur Ouine who has the same ability to read into the thoughts of those who come to him, but who uses this ability for evil purposes, to undermine the spirits of his victims. When Monsieur Ouine says: 'I am consumed by curiosity',[36] he uses his curiosity to exercise power over the souls whose lives he has sought to control without their knowing the power he has over them: 'The safety of these souls is in my hands, and they don't know it, I would hide it from them or reveal it, in turn.'[37]

But when we return to the dialogue between the priest and the countess, we know that her armour has been breached and she is now a broken woman, needing to confess and be absolved of the cumulative grievances of the previous years. The priest finds himself accusing her of lack of love, saying that God will break her and that her heart has become hard. As they fire verbal arrows at each other, she is being emotionally stripped of her past, accumulated bitterness, and when he suddenly becomes emotional himself with the force of his words and the tension in the situation, she softens and tries to console him. During the conversation, the priest has gained spiritual assurance and speaks words of conviction to her. She pours out her anger towards God, which the priest does not condemn as blasphemy, but turns into words of comfort:

> Madame […] if our God were a pagan god or the god
> of intellectuals – and for me it comes to much the
> same – He might fly to His remotest heaven and our
> grief would force Him down to earth again. But you
> know that our God came to be among us. Shake your
> fist at Him, spit in His face, scourge Him, and finally
> crucify Him: what does it matter? *My daughter, it's
> already been done to Him* (134).[38]

He had earlier in their conversation during a long speech to her stated: 'Hell is not to love any more' (128), and she now wants him to repeat this, which he does, then he adds in poetic terms beyond what he believes to be his capabilities: 'As long as we remain in this life we can still deceive ourselves, think that we love by our own will, that we love independently of God. But we're like madmen stretching out hands to clasp the moon reflected in water' (134). In the meantime she had taken out a medallion containing a lock of her child's hair, which she now suddenly and impulsively flings into the fire and which the priest vainly tries to extricate for her. She is chastened and succumbs to the need for confession and absolution.

When he leaves her, she is at peace. The next day he receives a letter from her which is crucial in reflecting the vital importance of recapturing the innocence of childhood. In her letter she writes: 'I have lived in the most terrible solitude, alone with the desperate memory of a child. And it seems to me that another child has brought me to life again. I hope you won't be annoyed with me for regarding you as a child. Because you are! May God keep you one for ever!' (137).

The entire conversation involving her cleansing from the past and her discovery of peace has led to the point that the priest who has gained the power of convincing exhortation and the confidence to launch an assault on her demons, has also demonstrated the directness and innocence of a child in her eyes. Both of them have had to undergo the tension of the conversation in order to discover their true childlike natures. The countess has recovered her childhood before she then dies, in the middle of the following night, leaving the priest stunned, but now articulate and confident in the strength that has been given him. Despite his growing illness which means that he has at last decided to go to Lille for treatment he deals confidently with the governess, Louise, who now has to leave the château, and with Séraphita who has found him unconscious by the roadside and is herself very much chastened.

At this point, the priest has what he calls 'a strange meeting' that is totally new in his experience and is vital to our consideration (183). He meets Olivier, the nephew of the count and a soldier in the Foreign Legion soon to return to duty, and with him he strikes up a very natural, open friendship. The priest finds exhilaration in a brief and exciting motor cycle ride on Olivier's motorcycle. He feels rejuvenated, he laughs and is able to listen with equanimity to Olivier's severe criticisms of the Church. He responds naturally to them and Olivier feels that the priest who had been seriously criticised by his uncle, the count, is like any normal human being.

Apart from the criticisms that Olivier makes of the Church, which have already been considered, Olivier is able to say important things to the priest about prayer. While the priest at one point earlier in the story says that he spends the whole night praying, he admits his great difficulties in the habit of prayer. Olivier latches on to the phrase 'the habit of prayer' and expresses the view that such a term implies 'a continual anxiety with regard to prayer. It is the perpetual dread of fear, the *fear of fear*, that shapes the face of a brave man'. Looking at the priest, he adds: 'Your face [...] looks worn by prayer' (190-191).[39] He has shrewdly sensed that the priest's difficulty with prayer is due to the fact that it has become a habit that he cannot easily sustain, a worry that is wearing him out and an indication that in this respect he has fallen into the trap of official religion that expects its priests to be men of prayer and imposes the habit on them. This will be explored further later.

When Olivier takes his leave, he tells the priest: 'You're a good lad [...] I wouldn't like any priest but you around when I was dying.' And he spontaneously kisses the priest on both cheeks (195).

Enough indications have become evident to suggest the vital importance of recapturing the spontaneity and innocence of children.

The priest has shown the degree of tolerance and genuine acceptance of the sincerity of the other's remarks to suggest that, with his new-found confidence and non-judgemental attitude to the problems of others, he has grown towards the ideal that Bernanos is seeking for him.

The word 'grace' does not feature in the early part of the story and first appears on page 92. Thereafter grace comes increasingly to the fore, strangely enough as Ambricourt's self-confidence increases and he realises that God is using him to help souls in distress. Joy also comes increasingly into his life as he discovers his youthful spirit and appreciates the views of others without judging them harshly as he had at the start of his conversation with the countess. Both these qualities may be associated with the attitudes of children. While not all children enjoy a happy childhood and many of Bernanos' characters endure a difficult time as children, Bernanos associates childhood with innocent acceptance, simplicity and dependence. At one point in the priest's conversations with Torcy, the latter speaks rapturously of the virtues of Our Lady, Her innocence, of Her 'child-eyes', Her total simplicity and Her motherly pity. She is 'though a mother, by grace, Mother of all grace, our little youngest sister' (166). She is both Mother and youngest sister, a child in Torcy's eyes. Children are naturally dependent on their mothers. The child Jesus was no exception.

Even Saint Francis of Assisi, whom Torcy mentions in the same paragraph as his fulsome reference to the Virgin Mary, was not free of sin as the Virgin was, but he is still included among the great saints whom Bernanos sets as an example to the Church. Francis also features in *Les grands cimetières sous la lune* as advocating the way of Poverty. As he does so, he says that he, Bernanos, will lead the way: 'I will throw myself into it', Bernanos writes, echoing the spirit of Francis and a few lines later 'Forward!'.[40]

The words 'I will throw myself into it' are an echo of the words in one of Ambricourt's final conversations before he leaves for Lille, a conversation with Chantal in which, much chastened, she still maintains that she will continue to 'do evil out of spite'. The advice he gives to her would certainly not have been given previously, but in his newly-found confidence he is able to say: 'And when you do […] you'll discover God. Go ahead for all you're worth, the walls are bound to fall in the end, and every breach shows a patch of sky' (200).

The phrase 'Go ahead for all you're worth' is the translator's rendering of the French '*Jetez-vous en avant tant que vous voudrez*'. The French phrase '*Jetez-vous en avant*' or slight grammatical variations but with the same verb, occurs many times in Bernanos' writings. In *La joie*, the saintly Chantal, in her conversation with a much chastened Father Cénabre and using the same verb, regrets that she had not yet taken the leap forward of faith.[41] Similarly, in *Sous le soleil de Satan*, but using the synonym, 's'élancer', Sabiroux, describing Donissan, regrets not having the latter's boldness in the Faith in the words: 'I would have wished I had taken a leap of faith forward, face dangers, perhaps martyrdom'.[42] In his early novel *Un mauvais rêve*, Olivier de Mainville, writing to his aunt, commends his employer, Madame Alfieri, for her ability to 'throw herself forward, to confront things'.[43] In *Les grands cimetières sous la lune* the phrase also occurs as 'se jeter en avant' in his discussion of the heroism of the medieval king, Saint Louis.[44] In *La grande peur des bien-pensants*, his exhortation to the French is 'What does being right matter? We must throw ourselves into it.'[45] The critic Michel Estève exactly repeats Ambricourt's words to Chantal in his Postface to the French edition of the same text,[46] and reiterates the spirit of Bernanos' thought earlier, but changes the verb to '*s'élancer en avant*', pointing out that Bernanos, in wishing to recapture the heroic spirit of the past, is hoping to be able to make a great leap forward in faith into the future.[47] In *Les enfants humiliés*, his diary of events in 1939-1940, he claims that the fate of the French nation can only be solved in the same terms by 'taking a leap of faith forward'.[48]

The frequency of such references and ideas reflects Bernanos' conviction of the vital importance of total commitment and heroism, both in the revival of the national spirit and of the individual's Christian's belief and practice. It is the heroism to which Olivier refers in his meeting with Ambricourt, the heroism of Joan of Arc. It is the childlike spirit of uninhibited, impulsive commitment in faith that one must leap forward into the unknown.

However, Joan of Arc is only a little less important to Bernanos than St Thérèse of Lisieux who acts as his model of childlike simplicity and total commitment to faith and the life of Christ. In her autobiography, *The Story of a Soul*, she tells how she desires to be called 'Sainte Thérèse of the Child Jesus'.[49] She is already mentioned in *Sous le soleil de Satan* as one who has prolonged moments of ecstasy[50] and she is also the model for Chantal in *La joie* who early in the novel describes herself as 'the favourite little girl of Saint Theresa'.[51] Chantal has such prolonged ecstasies, though she wishes to hide them and regrets being observed during one of these periods of ecstasy by the lustful chauffeur, Fiodor. These moments of private ecstasy contrast clearly with her practical attentions to the work of the household. Though St Thérèse is not mentioned in *Diary of a Country Priest*, her spirit pervades the concluding pages of the novel. But in *Les grands cimetières sous la lune* she features at significant moments. During the work, an agnostic takes the opportunity, on the feast day of St Thérèse to launch an attack on the Church whom he addresses as '*dévots et dévotes*' and warns the Church that, while they are not paying attention to the unbelievers, the unbelievers are certainly watching them.[52] Bernanos then says that St Theresa 'preached the spirit of childhood' and he continues: 'The spirit of childhood can do good and evil. It is not a spirit of accepting injustice.'[53] In this vein, he continues by asking what she would make of their politicians and arbiters of moral behaviour.[54] In the epilogue to *The Story of a Soul*, in which the account is changed to a third-person verdict on her life and, at one point, on what she meant by the term 'Little Way' that she applies to her life's course, she defines it as 'the way of spiritual childhood, the way of trust and complete self-surrender'.[55] But lest it be thought that this is the recipe for a passive life, earlier in her account of her life she describes Joan of Arc as one of France's special heroines[56] and shortly before her death she speaks again of her in words that have special significance for Bernanos' later creativity, when she writes: 'Like St Agnes and St Cecilia, I want to offer my neck to the executioner's sword, and like Joan of Arc, murmur the name of Jesus at the burning stake.'[57] Again heroism and martyrdom are to the fore, as is the spirit of childhood which will be further developed in our consideration of Bernanos' last work, *Dialogues des Carmélites*, which will complete our study.

At this moment, however, we return to key moments towards the end of *Diary of a Country Priest* when the priest has arrived in Lille, undergone medical examination, accepted the reality of his fate that he has cancer of the stomach and knows that he is to die. He writes in his diary many thoughts about childhood and the need to recapture its spirit. His spirit has been transformed. He has gained confidence and joy, realism and tolerance. He has accepted his past and knows no bitterness, and can feel happiness in the 'small joys that release me' (230). He then in a new entry talks of his attitude to death:

> I do not turn my back on death, neither do I confront
> it bravely as M. Olivier surely would. I have tried
> to open my eyes to death in all the simplicity of
> surrender, yet with no secret wish to soften or disarm.
> Were the comparison less foolish, I would look upon
> death as I did on [...] Mlle Chantal. Alas, one would
> need also to *become as a little child* (230).[58]

The association of the acceptance of death with simplicity and surrender are the qualities of a little child whose simplicity has not been destroyed by consciousness of impending loss or by the soldier's tradition of courageous confrontation.

As death approaches, he is ministered to by his friend and former fellow seminarian, Louis Dufréty who had abandoned the priesthood and is living unmarried with a woman. The third-person account of his death, sent to Torcy by Dufréty, relates how there is very little time for a priest to be summoned to give the last rites. He asks Dufréty to give him the last rites which he does, though Dufréty is no longer in the priesthood. Whereas previously our priest would have balked at a procedure that is contrary to Church law, his attitude, serene and accepting, is 'Does it matter? Grace is […] everywhere' (234). These last words of the novel are not at all unexpected. The last words in Ambricourt's diary are in the same vein. He accepts that during his life he has hated himself, but 'True grace is to forget. Yet if pride could die in us, the supreme grace would be to love oneself in all simplicity – as one would love any one of those who themselves have suffered and loved in Christ' (232). While accepting that pride might well remain in his spirit, he has come to love himself in Christ. Christ is the last word in his diary account. Grace has gradually replaced all sense of embattlement and defeat. He has learned the simplicity of a child and he is at peace.

Dialogues des Carmélites

But our study is not yet complete. In his last work, the drama *Dialogues des Carmélites*, completed just before his death, Bernanos develops his thoughts on heroism and the simple purity of St Thérèse to the full. The work contains all the concepts that Bernanos had pursued throughout his life. It is set at the time of the French Revolution. A young aristocratic girl from a rich family, Blanche, who has led a comfortable life seeks a life of heroism and self-sacrifice in a Carmelite order. She clearly wishes to be identified with the sufferings of the crucified Christ when she asks to be known in the order as Sister Blanche of the Death Agony of Christ, without fully understanding its implications, having just been warned by the Prioress for wishing to 'throw herself into the life without restraint',[59] a final appearance of this key phrase that Bernanos has introduced so often into his work. Blanche has many of the qualities of St Thérèse, though of course the latter who lived later is not mentioned in the play. While St Thérèse was a Carmelite nun and was admitted to the order before the usual age after her constant pressure to be admitted, Blanche does not have her single-minded fearlessness. She has the saint's simplicity and is advised by the Prioress never to lose this. The Prioress acts as a mouthpiece for very many of the ideas that Bernanos has been advocating, pointing out in the same speech that God is glorified not only by his saints, martyrs and heroes, but by the poor (47), something that Blanche after her sheltered upbringing is now learning. The Prioress also reminds the nuns that their chief purpose by which they stand or fall is prayer (59), a clear statement that Bernanos has learned after Ambricourt's struggle to learn how to pray properly. Blanche suffers from fear, a matter pointed out to her by her brother when he visits her in the nunnery and tries to persuade her to return home with him. He believes that she wishes only to stay among the Carmelites for fear of the challenges of returning home and he reiterates the need for total courage to combat fear: 'One has to risk fear just as one risks death, the real courage is in this risk' (73). But when the Carmelites are in danger of their life under the Revolution, Blanche flees and only changes her mind when she hears that the Sisters have been arrested and she insists on saving them, whilst also terrified of what might be in store (141). She has mistaken her role, which is not to save them, but to be with them to carry out the vow of allegiance they had taken (142). But she does not want to die and queries why the Sisters need her with them in order to die (143). However, the final note is of Blanche's self-sacrifice, joining the Sisters as they go to the guillotine.

Earlier, the Prioress had summarised so much of Bernanos' philosophy when she states the full significance of the Incarnation as the antidote to the evil in the world and describes Blanche's place in this:

> When the power of evil, which furthermore is nothing
> but appearance and illusion, is demonstrated with
> more brilliance that God becomes once again the little
> child in the cradle, as if in order to escape his own
> justice, the demands of his own justice, so to speak,
> in order to cheat it….Isn't it the gentle childhood of
> the Lord, in the person of our poor little girl, Blanche,
> that risks keeping up this demonstration of heroism?
> [...] I have always willingly believed that if strength is a
> virtue, there is not enough of this virtue for everybody,
> that the strong are only strong at the expense of the
> weak and that weakness will ultimately be reconciled
> and glorified in universal redemption (127-128).

It is not only the innocence and simplicity of the little child that are essential, but her weakness. This confirms what the Prioress had said earlier in the play when Blanche had come seeking a heroic life (31). 'What He (God) wishes to put to the test is not your strength, but your weakness' (31). Just as St Paul writes: 'My power is made perfect in weakness' (2 Cor. 12.9), it is weakness and vulnerability that are the characteristics of true children of God, in Bernanos' credo. It is when we know our weakness and still take the leap of faith, as Blanche finally does, that true likeness to Christ is achieved. This is what Ambricourt had found in the course of *Diary of a Country Priest*. While he always knows his weakness, only after his conversation with the countess does he find the joy of God's strength and discover that his weakness is in fact his strength.

Both he and Blanche have become as little children, just as Jesus has called them when He says: 'Unless you change and become like little children, you will never enter the kingdom of God' (Mt.18.3).

But they arrive by different routes, Blanche by an initial wrong idea of the meaning of strength, the priest by his initial inability to realise the strength that is available to him in his weakness.

Thus when Bernanos writes to the girl in Brazil that she should 'remain faithful to childhood. Never become an adult',[60] he is expressing his most heartfelt wish. He knows however that her adulthood will come, just as his has, and that childhood is vulnerable. His work is pervaded by this double vision of the ideal and the real. He believes that the Church has achieved a corrupt adulthood and has lost the simplicity and innocence that it must and can regain. Perhaps Bernanos was destined to remain an individualist and an idealist, but his vision of perfection remains one that the children and Church of God must learn and take to heart.

This article was first published in *The Heythrop Journal,* March 2015.

Endnotes

1   Albert Béguin (ed.), *Bernanos par lui-même* (Écrivains de toujours, éditions du seuil, 1961), my translation, 96.

2   Georges Bernanos, *Monsieur Ouine* (Le Castor Astral, 2008), 230. My translation. There is a translation by Geoffrey Dunlop, *The Open Mind* (The Bodley Head,1945).

3   Georges Bernanos, *Sous le soleil de Satan* (Le Castor Astral, 2008), 153. My translation. There is a translation by J.C. Whitehouse, *The Star of Satan* (The Bodley Head, 1927).

4   Bernanos, *Satan*, 211.

5   Bernanos, *Satan*, 219.

6   Bernanos, *Satan*, 244.

7   Georges Bernanos, *L'imposture* (Plon, 1929), 43. My translation.

8   Georges Bernanos, *La joie* (Plon, 1929), 27. My translation. There is a translation by Louise Varese, *Joy* (The Bodley Head, 1948).

9   Bernanos, *La joie*, 41.

10 Bernanos, *La joie*, 95.

11 Bernanos, *Ouine*, 325.

12 Gerda Blumenthal, *The Poetic Imagination of Georges Bernanos* (Baltimore, The Johns Hopkins Press, 1965), 22.

13 Bernanos, *Satan*, 25.

14 Bernanos, *Satan*, 200.

15 Bernanos, *Satan*, 329.

16 Bernanos, *Satan*, 380.

17 Bernanos, *L'imposture*, 35.

18 Georges Bernanos, *Les grands cimetières sous la lune* (Plon, 1938), 232. My translation. There is a translation by Pamela Morris, *A Diary of my Times* (The Bodley Head, 1938).

19 Bernanos, *Cimetières*, 232

20 Gerald Vann, *The Divine Pity* (Collins Fontana, 1956), 37.

21 Bernanos, *Cimetières*, 137.

22 Bernanos, *Cimetières*, 138.

23 Georges Bernanos, *La grande peur des bien-pensants* (Gallimard, 1969), 360. My translation.

24 Bernanos, *Cimetières*, 229.

25 Georges Bernanos, *Diary of a Country Priest (Journal d'un curé de campagne)* translated by Pamela Morris (The Bodley Head, 1937), 193. From now on, as this is the main text of this study, future references to it will be given in brackets in the text.

26 Bernanos, *Cimetières*, 227.

27 Bernanos, *L'imposture*, 74.

28 Michael R. Tobin, *Georges Bernanos: The Theological Source of his Art* (McGill-Queen's University Press, 2007), 117-118.

29 Vann, *Divine Pity*, 107.

30 Bernanos, *Cimetières*, 10.

31 Malcolm Scott, *Journal d'un curé de campagne: Critical Guides to French Texts* (London: Grant & Cutler, 1997), 57.

32 Robert Speaight, *Georges Bernanos* (London: Collins & Harvill Press, 1973), 138.

33 Scott, *Journal*, 75.

34 Speaight, *Bernanos*,150.

35 See note 1.

36 Bernanos, *Ouine*, 325.

37 Bernanos, *Ouine*, 327.

38 Author's italics.

39 Author's italics.

40 Bernanos, *Cimetières*, 229-230.

41 Bernanos, *La joie*, 219.

42 Bernanos, *Satan*, 305.

43 Georges Bernanos, *Un mauvais rêve* (Plon, 1951), 9. My translation. There is a translation by W.J. Strachan, *Night is Darkest* (The Bodley Head, 1953).

44 Bernanos, *Cimetières*, 304-305.

45 Bernanos, *Peur*, 120.

46 Bernanos, *Peur*, 386.

47 Bernanos, *Peur*, 383.

48 Georges Bernanos, *Les enfants humiliés* (Gallimard, 1949), 75-76. My translation.

49 Sainte Thérèse de Lisieux, *The Story of a Soul,* (*Histoire d'une âme*) translated by Michael Day (Rockford, IL: Tan Books, 1997), 46.

50 Bernanos, *Satan*, 212.

51 Bernanos, *La joie*, 32.

52 Bernanos, *Cimetières*, 214-215.

53 Bernanos, *Cimetières*, 227.

54 Bernanos, *Cimetières*, 229.

55 Thérèse, *Soul*, 214.

56 Thérèse, *Soul*, 47.

57 Thérèse, *Soul*, 198.

58 Author's italics.

59 Georges Bernanos, *Dialogues des Carmélites* (Éditions du Seuil, 1996), 33. My translation. There is a translation by Michael Legat, *The Fearless Heart* (The Bodley Head, 1961). As this is a major text in this study, all further text references will be in brackets in the text.

60 See note 1.

The Unseen Hook
and the Invisible Line
Tradition, faith and commitment in Evelyn Waugh's *Brideshead Revisited*[1] and subsequent novels

In an article in *The Observer* in 2007 a writer commenting on the scriptwriter Andrew Davies' adaptation of *Brideshead Revisited* for the cinema, referred to Davies' comment on the previous 'monolithic' television adaptation of the novel in 1981:

> All anyone remembers is Charles and Sebastian
> swanning around Oxford and, certainly to Evelyn
> Waugh, that was not the main part of the book. The
> crux of the book is [...] Julia Flyte's giving up Charles
> for God. It is the religious crisis that the book is
> working towards.[2]

Davies had already said much the same thing in 2002 when he said that the book begs the question: 'Is God more important than love? It's a Catholic novel.'[3]

It is the purpose of this study to consider from *Brideshead Revisited* onwards the evidence of Waugh's religious stance as expressed in these his later novels. In his much later novel *The Ordeal of Gilbert Pinfold* Waugh says of his protagonist, the writer Pinfold: 'He regarded his books as objects which he had made, things quite external to himself to be used and judged by others.'[4] Biographical references are ancillary to how Waugh, the artist, exploits his experience in his works. Even in his letters he says very little about his feelings expressed in his novels. The artist speaks through his work which even then only expresses what he chooses to say and is often eloquent for what he omits.

Brideshead Revisited

Certainly early in *Brideshead Revisited* when Charles Ryder becomes infatuated with Sebastian and their first years as undergraduates at Oxford are given full treatment, there is no indication of the religious crisis that will eventually develop from Charles' involvement with Sebastian's family. He is writing about an aristocratic Catholic family owning a country estate, Brideshead, based firmly on Waugh's experience of his close associations with the country estate of Madresfield near Malvern. Charles' return visit to Brideshead during the war reminds him of the events that unfold since he first meets Sebastian in 1923 and which continue until shortly before the outbreak of war.

The first indication of problems underlying the life of the family comes when Sebastian first takes Charles to Brideshead and describes the house as 'not [...] my house, but where my family lives'.[5] Charles realises that Sebastian is unsympathetic to what his family, especially his mother, stands for. It emerges that the father has settled abroad, that the mother, Lady Marchmain, exercises a spiritual dominance over the family. The oldest of the four children, Lord Brideshead, who is a fervent, orthodox Roman Catholic, never fulfils his earlier aspiration to become a Jesuit. He assumes particular importance at the time of crisis towards the end of the novel. The second oldest is Sebastian who is a sceptic and blasé cynic and, like his father, rejects the enervating religious influence of his mother. The mother knows full well that her husband and Sebastian in their different ways both fled from her dominating piety. Gradually Sebastian descends into acute alcoholism but finds redemption later., though he lives in Morocco and rather fades out of the main plot following his estrangement from Charles who is unable to help him out of his alcoholism. Then there are the girls. Julia whom Charles first meets when she is eighteen, is at that time blasé and worldly, described by Sebastian as 'semi-heathen'.[6] Much later when she has learned from experience, she describes her mother thus: 'All through her life, mummy had all the sympathy of everyone except those she loved.'[7] The youngest of the family is Cordelia, a very pious child, like her eldest brother and her mother. She is to play a key role as she grows and tempers piety with experience.

With the main characters in place, the stage is set for the religious issues to take their course. There appear to be three main threads. Firstly, there is the agnostic Charles who questions the piety of the devout members of the family and their adherence to correct Catholic doctrine and practice. In a conversation with Lord Brideshead he says: 'D'you know, Bridey, if I ever felt for a moment like becoming a Catholic, I should only have to talk to you for five minutes to be cured.'[8] In a previous conversation with Lord Brideshead, after the latter, in discussing Sebastian, has said rather unusually for him: 'I believe God prefers drunkards to a lot of respectable people.' Charles, after asking him 'Why bring God into everything?', goes on to say: 'It seems to me that without your religion Sebastian would have the chance to be a happy and healthy man.'[9] When, at the end of the novel after Lord Marchmain has returned home to die and Lord Brideshead insists on calling the priest to hear his confession and give him absolution, Charles acts as the critical observer, supporting Lord Marchmain's refusal to see the priest and questioning the entire basis of the need for the priest to be involved. Talking of the dying man, he says:

> He has [...] to be contrite and wish to be reconciled
> [...] But only God knows whether he has really made
> an act of will; the priest can't tell; and if there isn't a
> priest there, and he makes the act of will alone, that's

as good as if there were a priest. And it's quite possible
that the will may still be working when a man is too
weak to make any outward sign of it.

True confession has to be inward and God would know whether or not it is genuine. 'What is the priest for?', asks Charles.[10] But the tradition and habit are too strong in the family for his argument to have any effect, and ironically, his reasoning and critical attitude which she shares at the time helps towards Julia's eventual decision not to marry him.

In the development of the religious issue, Charles' critical position highlights the intense piety of the devout members of the family and their adherence to the letter of Catholic doctrine and practice, which is the second thread to be considered. His conversations with Lady Marchmain emphasise the strengths and weaknesses of her position, her popularity with outsiders, her charming attempt to take Charles into her confidence and also make him into a Catholic, and her ultimate inflexibility that alienates two of the men in her family. But apart from Charles' involvement, Waugh obviously has fun in describing the situation of Rex Mottram, Julia's lover and later husband, in his desire to become a Catholic to satisfy the needs of her tradition. Yet he demonstrates his total inability to understand the significance and detail of the catechism for which he hurriedly undergoes training and to grasp that his previous marriage, long since over, and his current affair are obstacles to his marriage that have to be overcome. While enjoying the more hilarious moments, Waugh is also indicating the strength of the Catholic moral stance over the more lax mores of the post-First War era. And when Lady Marchmain has died, Lord Brideshead continues to enforce Catholic principles, towards Julia and Charles' affair and in the closing days of Lord Marchmain's life.

It is the still young, but maturing Cordelia, echoing the words of her mother, who represents the third and the most significant religious assertion, God's sovereignty over all events. This is the most convenient point to recall the entire background to the Catholic dimension referred to by Andrew Davies above.

Waugh had been converted to Catholicism fifteen years before he wrote *Brideshead Revisited*. He was received into the Catholic Church on 29 September 1930. Waugh claimed that 'in the present phase of European history the essential issue is no longer between Catholicism [...] and Protestantism [...] but between Christianity and Chaos'.[11] The rational nature of his decision is expressed many years later in an interview in which Waugh gives as his reason for his 'conversion' 'simply a fact of recognising a plausible rational system, of following the arguments with proof of the historic truth of Christianity'.[12]

Waugh never thought of this transformation in his outlook as a 'conversion'. In *The Ordeal of Gilbert Pinfold* Waugh writes of his author Pinfold, the very expression of himself: 'He had been received into the Church – 'conversion' suggests an event more sudden and emotional than his calm acceptance of the propositions of his faith',[13] suggesting a matter-of-fact acceptance of the essential tenets of faith and commitment to a new way of life. Waugh's reception into the Catholic Church, though expressed in markedly intellectual terms, has all the hallmarks of an outright rejection of the moral worldliness of his age. It is interesting and surprising that it was fifteen years later that his change was fully expressed in *Brideshead Revisited*. But it was written after years of conflict throughout the world in which the decline of civilisation into chaos had been fully evident.

The influence of G.K. Chesterton is most important in the novel. It is Cordelia who highlights this. In a letter Waugh comments that 'the last conversation with Cordelia gave the theological clue'.[14] She is still only fifteen when, in her final conversation with Charles in which she speaks of the current fortunes of the family following the death of her mother, she mentions the closing of their chapel and goes on to talk of the way in which three of her family, her father, Sebastian and Julia, have 'gone' from the faith. 'But God won't let them go for long, you know.'[15] And she recalls a moment on the evening when the family first becomes aware of Sebastian's serious drinking problem, when her mother reads from one of the Father Brown stories. Waugh allows Lady Marchmain to introduce the very theme that lies at the heart of the novel and that arose from Waugh's reading of one of Chesterton's stories, The *Queer Feet*, quoted by Lady Marchmain and later reiterated by Cordelia in her conversation with Charles.

In the story, Father Brown is in a hotel where the club of The Twelve True Fishermen (surely an echo of the Twelve Disciples) are celebrating their annual club dinner to which, as always, they have brought their famous set of fish knives and forks, their insignia. During the meal this immensely valuable cutlery is stolen, but is recovered by the ingenuity and skill of Father Brown from the hands of the master criminal, Flambeau, who has gained access to the dinner by dressing in the black garb appropriate to both the role of a waiter and of one of the members of the club. Father Brown is able to recover the cutlery from Flambeau as the latter is about to leave the hotel, but he does not apprehend him physically, allowing him to escape. Father Brown says that 'He has made me a fisher of men' and, when asked if he has caught the thief, explains in the crucial words: 'I caught him, with an unseen hook and an invisible line which is long enough to let him wander to the ends of the world, and still to bring him back with a twitch upon the thread.'[16] It is as if Father Brown is fulfilling a divine mission, yet able to bide his time, knowing that the master criminal who features in many of these stories can be hauled back to his just punishment.

The significance of the words recalled by Cordelia[17] is that God, through his Church, is able to hold the wanderers in his power, so that, though they wander for a while, He will inevitably draw them back into the orbit of His Church. She is reflecting the spirit of the earlier thought of Lord Brideshead that God loves the drunkards more than many respectable people when the 'drunkard' is Sebastian who has been brought up within the Church and is forever loved and sought by God. Much later Cordelia, from her experience of social work, speaks to Charles about Sebastian in his late stage of alcoholism: 'I've seen others like him, and I believe they are very near and dear to God.'[18] We have already long before heard that Sebastian out in Tangier has befriended a destitute German demonstrating his newly found spirit of humility and self-sacrifice, expressed with wry modesty in his words to Charles: 'It has to be someone pretty hopeless to need looking after by me.'[19] Though the events at this point in the novel are taking place well before the war, the fact that the novel was written when it was and the nationality of the man he is helping surely are striking a blow for the spirit of charity and reconciliation, echoed much later in the behaviour of Guy Crouchback in *Unconditional Surrender*.

It certainly seems as if true religion issuing in a sense of practical service and vocation is emerging from behind the appearance of adherence to doctrine and tradition and confirming their value. Cordelia, in one of the final thoughts in the first part of the novel, speaks of the strength of vocation as the essence of true religion: 'If you haven't a vocation, it's no good however much you want to be; and if you have a vocation, you can't get away from it, however much you hate it.'[20] This theme will be developed later. It seems as if Waugh is starting to set the scene for the final stage in this drama, the doomed love of Charles and Julia and the religious crisis which, in Andrew Davies' words, 'the book is working towards'.

Charles and Julia have both married, Julia to Rex Mottram and Charles to Celia, the sister of a friend. Both marriages are unhappy. Rex has not given up his affair and Julia's baby is stillborn. She has wanted to bring the baby up as a Catholic, despite the fact that she has turned away from religion, such is the tug on 'the unseen hook and the invisible line', the force of tradition in this Catholic family.

She had thought: 'That's one thing I can give her. It doesn't seem to have done me much good, but my child shall have it.'[21] Charles has become a famous artist, and he and Julia lose sight of each other for ten years, though they keep up to date with each other's life and their love has started to grow *in absentia*. He has travelled much with his work and publications, and his wife has been unfaithful. When he and Julia meet again, their love grows, divorce and re-marriage are planned, such is her estrangement from the Catholic doctrine that would have forbidden it.

After their relationship has become public knowledge, the moment of greatest importance for Julia's ultimate decision takes place one evening when Lord Brideshead announces his own engagement, but says that his future bride would not want to live in a house where Charles and Julia 'choose to live in sin'.[22] Julia, outraged by her brother's pomposity and pettiness, rushes out to the fountain in the garden where the fateful conversation with Charles takes place that becomes so crucial to their future. Hysterically she pours out her feelings which swing between two poles of thought. Firstly, there is her family's Catholic tradition, with frantic, obsessive references to virtually all the members of her family past and present including the nanny, imagining how they all are reacting to her 'living in sin, with sin, always the same'. 'Poor Julia,' they say, 'she can't go out. She's got to take care of her sin [...] Julia's so good to her little, mad sin.'[23] She is convinced at that moment that her whole life is exposed to the glare of her traditions and that she is judged accordingly. But not only by them. Also by Christ.

> Mummy dying with it (sin); Christ dying with it,
> nailed hand and foot; hanging over the bed in the
> night-nursery; hanging year after year in the dark
> little study at Farm Street [...] hanging at noon,
> high among the crowds and the soldiers; no comfort
> except a sponge of vinegar and the kind words of a
> thief; hanging for ever; never the cool sepulchre and

the grave clothes spread on the stone slab […] always
the midday sun and the dice clicking for the seamless
coat.[24]

The image of her mother's piety and sufferings for the 'sin' of her family become merged with images of the Crucifixion where for the first time she sees her sin as identified with the sins that put Christ on the Cross. And finally, she returns to her own condition, seeing the body of Christ wrapped up and taken away like her stillborn baby before she had had a chance to see her.

While she then recovers her poise and proceeds with determination to the arrangements for the divorce on which she has set her heart, Charles knows that that moment by the fountain is the decisive moment in their relationship, the beginning of the end, when she 'wept her heart out for the death of her God'.[25] He knows that she sees God in Christ dying on the Cross and her 'living in sin' as identified with the sin for which Christ died.

When the crisis occurs over whether her father, a convinced opponent of the Catholic religion, should be confronted with the priest she is the one despite her previous doubts who finally summons Father Mackay who is prepared to take a very gentle line with Lord Marchmain. Then the unexpected happens. When it looks as if her dying, semi-conscious father will again refuse absolution, Charles finds himself, despite his agnosticism and his previous severe criticism of the procedure, praying: 'O God, if there is a God, forgive him his sins, if there is such a thing as sin.' His prayer is hedged about with the tentative suggestion that God and sin might not exist, a confirmation of his previous scepticism, a desire that forgiveness should happen only for the sake of Julia. But interestingly, his next prayer is much more affirmative of the reality and presence of God. 'God forgive him his sins' and 'Please God, make him accept your forgiveness'.[26] Having prayed his first prayer for Julia's sake, the obvious simple next step is to pray as he does the second time. And miraculously, Lord

Marchmain makes a feeble, but distinct sign of the cross! Having almost wriggled clear of the 'unseen hook and the invisible line' that has held the family in thrall and himself against his will, he is now reclaimed together with Julia.

So, when Julia then tells Charles of her decision never to marry him or even to see him again, she is unable to grasp that he can indeed understand. Her reasons are again informed by her frequent references to the influence of her family, but she is more convinced that her nature, filled with sin and her need of grace, needs the mercy of God. 'The worse I am, the more I need God. I cannot shut myself out from His mercy.' What is 'unforgivable' is 'to set up a rival good to God's'. Again, she reveals her dependence on her mother's example, her mother being the only one who had borne the burden of the sins of others for so long and who, with the other believing members of her family, had probably long prayed for them. Julia's final thought is very much one of making a bargain with God, that 'if I give up this one thing I want so much, however bad I am, he won't quite despair of me in the end'.[27]

While her decision appears very much like an insurance policy against the possibility of eventual damnation for the sins that trouble her and make her feel that she has 'always been bad', there is no doubt of its sincerity and the sacrifice to the life of loneliness to which she is consigning herself. We know later that she and Cordelia leave to serve in the war. She is indeed a changed person, convinced of her need of grace and of the sacrifice she has to make to claim it, going well beyond the acceptance of the family tradition that has held her for so long despite her earlier rejection of it.

Helena

Clearly, Waugh regards adherence to the new faith as a commitment to a new life. It is not a question of merely standing on the edge and observing intellectually. Not only are Cordelia and Julia believers, they are also actively committed to improving the human lot. Sebastian, too, though a recovering alcoholic, has committed himself to a life of service. The crucial importance of commitment beyond the initial acceptance of the teachings of the Church is developed very strongly in Waugh's novel *Helena*,[28] which he had started in 1945 before the publication of *Brideshead Revisited* and which appeared in 1950, a work which he considered his favourite novel, and which Waugh described to Ronald Knox as 'an unhistorical life of St Helena'.[29]

The novel is Waugh's most intentional statement about the truth of Christianity, about saintliness and about vocation as the heart of Christian discipleship. In a letter to John Betjeman who had doubted the saintliness of Helena, Waugh writes:

> Each individual has his own peculiar form of sanctity
> which he must achieve or perish. It is no good my
> saying: "I wish I were like Joan of Arc or St John of
> the Cross. I can only be St Evelyn Waugh – after God
> knows what experiences in purgatory." [30]

Waugh's conversion drives him to what he sees as its logical conclusion, that he must become a saint. He must discover the vocation by which God had determined how the individual was to be sanctified.

From the opening scene of the novel in her childhood Helena, mother of the emperor Constantine, shows a robust, down-to-earth spirit. She asks questions, determined to find her own answers and her own way. Marcias, her tutor, says very early on in answer to her constant enquiries: 'Sometimes, my child, you make startlingly intelligent observations.'[31] Her life takes her round the Roman Empire and she eventually comes to Rome where she hardly sees her son, Constantine, but steadily works her way towards her own faith. The Roman Empire, in Waugh's eyes mirroring the state of Europe following the Second World War, is in a state of confusion and decline, with casual slaughter and brutality the order of the day, but with various religions trying to assert themselves. She sees Rome as inward looking: 'Sometimes I wonder won't Rome ever go beyond the wall? Into the wild lands?' and she continues: 'Couldn't the wall be at the limits of the world and all men, civilised and barbarian, have a share in the City? Am I talking nonsense?'.[32] Her 'nonsense' is turned to advantage when she describes new supernatural cults, for example Mithras and Gnosticism, as 'bosh'. When she meets Marcias, now a Gnostic teacher, she cuts through his theories to ask the pertinent questions: 'When and where did all this happen? And how do you know?'.[33] When he describes her last question as 'a child's question', she replies: 'If I ever found a teacher, it would have to be one who called little children to him.' He almost makes the next point for her when he says: 'That […] is not the spirit of the time […] We know too much. We should have to forget everything and be born again to answer your questions.'[34] Though Waugh has since his conversion firmly relied on the teachings of the Church, here, through the mouth of Helena, he seems to be advocating a completely fresh start, a new approach to Faith through the direct, personal response of the *ingénue*, finding her own way, seeing, what Martin Stannard describes as 'the terrifying formlessness of the rational "adult" world when seen through the eyes of a "naif" '.[35]

In her conversations with the Christian tutor, Lactantius, her searching questions are directed at his faith. She wants to know the basis for her son, Constantine's, Christian allegiance. She asks: 'Was there a cross in the sky? Did my son see it? How did it get there?' Lactantius only knows that the Emperor has seen a vision. But 'Christianity […] cannot share a vision with anybody. Whenever it is free, it will conquer.' She feels that he never quite answers her questions, but that 'it all seems to make sense up to a point, and again beyond that point. And yet one can't pass the point […] Well, I am an old woman, too old to change now.'

Lactantius, however, sees that 'to be old was very heaven; to have lived in a Hope that defied reason'.[36] It signals the change that is to take place in Helena, a new vision of a faith and hope beyond reason, broached in her question 'Was there a cross in the sky?'. She realises that Constantine's 'faith' is far short of a true faith. It is as if Waugh himself is inserting his authorial wisdom when he says: 'The Supreme Deity recognised by Constantine was [...] far wide of the Christian Trinity.'[37] Helena has not yet reached that point, but she knows that her son's 'beliefs' represent 'Power without Grace'.[38] With the moral decay at the heart of the Empire, the vestiges of power survive. It is as if 'all the tiny mechanism of Power regularly revolved, like a watch still ticking on the wrist of a dead man'.[39]

We do not learn of an exact moment when Helena is converted, but we know of her constant seeking after truth and we learn quite suddenly that she has been baptised.[40] From now on, her course is very direct. She is not just going to 'nestle down in the cradle of universal respect and prepare her soul for the day when she would find herself wafted to heaven and royally received there'.[41] Her sanctity is an expression of her resolve to serve God in a concrete, practical way. As Waugh continues in his letter to Betjeman quoted above:

> I liked Helena's sanctity because it is in contrast to all
> that moderns think of as sanctity. She wasn't thrown
> to the lions, she wasn't a contemplative, she wasn't
> poor and hungry [...] She just discovered what it
> was God had chosen for her to do and did it [...] by
> going straight to the physical historical fact of the
> redemption.[42]

She vainly attempts to persuade her son to be baptised. In her conversation with Pope Sylvester, she hears him say what Waugh clearly felt to be the role of the Church, not only in Helena's day, but in our own time. 'The Church isn't a cult for a few heroes. It is the whole of fallen humanity redeemed.'[43] Helena, aware of the significance of the cross, asks him where the Cross is, 'the real one', not Constantine's artificial gold plated one on his standard. Sylvester replies by saying: 'If He (God) had wanted us to have it, no doubt

He would have given it to us. But He hasn't chosen to. He gives us enough.' But she shows her determination to find it. 'How do you know He doesn't want us to have it – the cross, I mean? I bet He's just waiting for one of us to go and find it – just at this moment when it's most needed.'[44] Writing to Maurice Bowra, Waugh places her search for the Cross within its historical context when he gives it precedence over the interest solely in the Incarnation at the time: 'Incarnation is no use without the Cross and vice versa. Everyone in the 4th century seems to have been concerned only with the Incarnation, except Helena.'[45]

So she sets off in the autumn of 326, when she is fifty-three years old. Her journey in her single-minded quest for the True Cross is characterised by good works and munificence. She takes over the grand project of the Archbishop of Jerusalem to uncover the Holy Sepulchre that had been burned down two hundred years previously under the Emperor Hadrian, and, despite appeals from her followers to abandon what they see as a futile quest as the difficulties mount up, with the guidance of the Wandering Jew whom she meets in a dream, she performs the miracle of finding the True Cross. Thus history merges with miracle and dream, creating an atmosphere commensurate with the spirit of the time of Christ. Yet another will be considered later in her encounter with the Three Wise Men when three bearded monks appear 'like the kings of old' prostrating themselves before the altar.[46] The author's final comment on her achievement is: 'Her work was finished. She had done what only the saints succeed in doing; what indeed constitutes their patent of sanctity. She had completely conformed to the will of God.'[47] As Stannard says comparing her position with Constantine's vague philosophy of establishing an empire in the East full of 'Divine Wisdom and Peace':[48] 'Constantine represents the eternal humanist fallacy. The only way to avoid it is through the remorseless fact of the lump of wood to which Christ was nailed in agony.'[49]

The Cross has in fact become the true centre of Helena's faith, just as it had become the true centre of Julia Flyte's experience, expressed in her monologue to Charles at the fountain.[50] It is as if both Helena and Julia are uttering what the worldly, outwardly superior Waugh is aware of in his innermost being, his own sin and failure to live up to the highest standards of goodness and spirituality. The rational Waugh, whose reception into the Church is expressed in the language of reason, is driven to kneel at the foot of the Cross, at least in the characters in these novels. Like Julia and Cordelia, Helena, in pursuing her dedicated quest to find the Cross, demonstrates the overriding importance of vocation in Waugh's conception of the nature of sainthood. Helena's dedication to her cause is her single-minded response to her need to find her own way to salvation, faith issuing in personal action. And her action would be nothing without her search to discover the very heart of the Faith, the Cross.

At the end of *Helena* Waugh extends his praise of her to enfold the whole of our present age in the arms of her achievement. 'Above all the babble of her age and ours, she makes one blunt assertion. And there alone lies Hope.' On the way to this assertion, Waugh cannot resist making a satirical comment on modern Britain: 'Britain for a time became Christian.'[51]

The Sword of Honour Trilogy[52]

The same critical view of the civilisation and values of Britain in the recent days of the war and its aftermath underlie his next major work, his *Sword of Honour* trilogy in which Waugh, through the eyes of his main character, Guy Crouchback, depicts a world in decline and decay. The first two novels, *Men at Arms* and *Officers and Gentlemen*, published in 1952 and 1955 respectively are not so overlaid with the religious aura of *Helena*, and spiritual values are now expressed through a depiction of moral and social attitudes, specifically in time of war, but extending to the spirit of the contemporary world in general. He sees the absence of honour early in the war, writing to Laura: 'I know that one goes into a war for reasons of honour and soon finds oneself called on to do very dishonourable things.'[53] Years later, in writing to his son Auberon, he sees, despite his love for him, evidence of his 'defective sense of honour'.[54] And he also sees another root cause of the decline of civilisation: 'I believe the sin the west is dying of to be Sloth.'[55] By describing what is for him largely a 'phoney war', a war in which much of his time is spent in clubs, hotels, drinking, socialising, or in training for postings that often lead to very little confrontation with the enemy, Waugh is allowing the reader to conclude that he is almost returning to the comic, satirical spirit of his early works. Only remotely do we hear of the debacle of Dunkirk. There is a botched escapade in Dakar and an ignominious evacuation from Crete. The litany includes incompetence, muddle, obfuscation, poor communication, even corruption, self-seeking, false reporting and sheer cowardice, with incompetence and cowardice rewarded.

Guy Crouchback, from an old established, highly respected Catholic family, is like Waugh in his mid thirties when war is declared, but he manages to enlist with the fictional Royal Corps of Halberdiers, most of whom seem to be ageing, but willing volunteers rather away from the main action of the war. Guy 'with his arid piety and emotional detachment' is largely a passive participant in events.[56] Others are preferred to him and are promoted above him, but he soldiers on, doing his duty, and in his final phase of the war he is in Yugoslavia, deeply frustrated and upset that he is unable to help the Jews and that 'he became the unwilling instrument in the subversion of a once Christian nation'.[57] Throughout he observes the prayer duties of a Catholic, but his religion only comes alive as a committed faith in the later stages of the third novel *Unconditional Surrender*, published in 1961.

His father, called Mr Crouchback throughout the trilogy, is 'an innocent, affable old man who had somehow preserved his good humour […] a mysterious and tranquil joy – throughout a life which to all outward appearances had been overloaded with misfortune'.[58] He is a strong presence in the background, representing the traditions of his Catholic family, charitable, willing to serve. Guy, the youngest son, has been married and is divorced. His wife, Virginia, described as 'bright and fashionable' is not a Catholic and, perhaps significantly, is not given a name when she is first mentioned, indicating that she fails to belong to the tradition of the family.[59] They have no children. She leaves Guy for another man and in the course of the novel has two other husbands. She is given a divorce, but Guy does not cease to love her and always considers her to be his wife. His failed marriage lives with him throughout and colours his mood and attitudes. It accounts largely for his withdrawn spirit. In the eight years before the war his spirit is benumbed. In confession he can only confess superficialities, never the deep grief, the residue of his failed love. 'Into that wasteland where his soul languished he need not, could not enter. There were no words to describe it […] There was nothing to describe, merely a void […] No cosmic struggle raged in his sad soul.'[60] He has lost his self-confidence. When he is trying to get into the army, he admits: 'But I'm not the pick of the nation […] I'm natural fodder. I've no dependants. I've no special skill in anything.'[61] Even though he is able to make contact again with his wife, albeit in an abortive attempt to make love to her, and is able to lay the ghost of his failed marriage, he still suffers from a sense of personal inadequacy. He describes himself as 'a good loser - at any rate an experienced one',[62] but he does achieve some distinction in his escape from Crete across the Mediterranean in one of his rare encounters with fighting. In this connection Waugh cannot resist a barbed satirical comment on Guy's frustrated passivity during his time in Yugoslavia when he writes to Laura, reflecting his own feelings as well as those of his main character: 'Yesterday we drove a great distance to see a battle.' Just a little later in the same letter he says: 'Today has lasted about a week already and it is only 4.15 p.m. We are like Chekhov characters.'[63] By now he would love to be able to do more to help those in need, especially the Jews: 'Our poor Jews stay in increasing distress.'[64]

Guy's attitudes have in fact changed quite considerably, a matter that must now be considered in detail seeing that he has been so negative in the early years of the war. The trilogy is now starting to fulfil what Waugh wrote in one of his letters to Clarissa Churchill, just after completing *Men at Arms* 'which won't show any shape until the end'.[65] Just after the start of *Unconditional Surrender* Mr Crouchback, who has not featured in the account for some time, is involved in a serious dispute with Guy. It is 1943, and Italy has just surrendered. Guy is at home with his father when he hears the news that the king of Italy had fled. Given that the unity of the country had now been destroyed by the King's flight, Guy criticises the Lateran Treaty of 1929, which the Papacy had signed with Mussolini under which the latter recognised the Pope's sovereign rights over a newly created Vatican City while the former acquiesced in the House of Savoy's occupation of the remaining Papal states. Guy feels that the Church sold out to the political powers and the Pope should have stayed his ground, not sullying his hands with political involvement.[66] However, his father disagrees strongly and in a letter to his son the following day, claims that the Church, by the creation of the Treaty, allowed the Faith to continue and countless souls to be saved.

> When you spoke of the Lateran Treaty did you
> consider how many souls may have been reconciled
> and have died at peace as a result of it? How many
> children may have been brought up in the Faith
> who might have lived in ignorance? Quantitative
> judgements don't apply. If only one soul was saved that
> is full compensation for any amount of loss of "face".[67]

When Mr Crouchback dies and Guy is alone with his thoughts at the funeral, he becomes aware of the vital importance of his father's words: 'Quantitative judgements don't apply.' He appreciates his father's supreme goodness and gives thanks for his life, himself very much aware that he himself had been near death in his crossing from Crete. As he prays, he remembers the direction in the spiritual manual *The Garden of the Soul* telling him: 'Put yourself in the presence of God.'[68] It is as if he is reporting for duty to God: 'I don't ask anything from you. I am here if you want me. I don't suppose I can be of any use, but if there is anything I can do, let me know', echoing a desperate earlier entry in his diary: 'My prayer is now only, "Here I am again. Show me what to do; help me to do it." '[69] He realises that God has not wanted him to ask nothing of him. 'He had commanded all men to ask.' He feels in the depths of his conscience that 'something would be required of him' and that 'he must be attentive to the summons when it came. They also served who only stood and waited.' He saw himself

> As one of the labourers in the parable who sat in the
> market place waiting to be hired and were not called
> into the vineyard until late in the day. They had their
> reward on an equality with the men who had toiled
> since dawn. One day he would get the chance to do
> some small service which only he could perform, for
> which he had been created. Even he must have his
> function in the divine plan. He did not expect a heroic
> destiny. Quantitative judgements did not apply.[70]

He knows that he now has a purpose, no matter how humble it might be and how late in the day. Until now he has not asked God what he must do. He still does not know, he must wait. At the back of his mind he is aware of his father's words in his letter: 'Quantitative judgements don't apply. If only one soul was saved that is full compensation for any amount of loss of "face".'[71] His calling is to be judged by its quality not quantity. It might be to help or even save one person only. There is a biblical precedent for this (Lk. 15) in the love for one person or thing only, either a lost coin, or lost sheep or lost son. And in the Jewish faith, reiterated in the novel *Schindler's Ark*, Oskar Schindler is inspired in his work of saving Jews from the gas chambers by the Talmudic verse: 'He who saves the life of one man saves the entire world.'[72] Nothing is too small to escape the love of God and the committed devotion of his servants. Sebastian after all shows his devotion to his new calling by helping one individual in need.

In depicting Guy as one who is now aware that he must seek God's will, Waugh is drawing a comparison with Helena who began her quest for God and continued to the end by *asking* the right questions and thus arriving at what His will for her might be. One is reminded of Waugh's words in his earlier letter to Betjeman referring to Helena's saintliness. 'She just discovered what it was that God had chosen for her to do and did it.'[73]

Guy knows that he has come late to his new calling. Again, we are reminded of Helena's words who, on arriving in Bethlehem, rests and dozes, with a vision of 'the swaddled child long ago and those three royal sages who had come from so far to adore him'. She says to herself: 'This is my day,' and she says to them: 'Like me [...] you were late in coming.'[74] Despite this and the disaster they had brought on countless innocent children by going to call on Herod first, they are accepted. 'Yet you came and were not turned away. You too found room before the manger.' Helena grants them a special place in her heart. 'You are my especial patrons [...] and patrons of all late-comers, of all who have a tedious journey to make to the truth.'[75]

Guy now belongs to the same tradition of those who come late to their special calling and are accepted, like Waugh himself, who, not born into a Catholic tradition, is received into the Church in his twenties. Guy comes from a Catholic family, but it is as if he has been estranged and now finds his calling, as does Julia Flyte, the rebel from the family tradition and Lord Marchmain, the one who had rejected the family Church tradition and returned very, very late to the Faith.

Guy finds his vocation in re-marrying his estranged wife, Virginia, and adopting the illegitimate child she has by the ne'er-do-well Trimmer whom she detests and rejects, the child that she needs to legitimise by returning to her first husband, Guy, who has never ceased to regard her as his wife and has never re-married, mindful of the Church's rule and in any case uninterested in any relationship other than with her. He can fulfil his duty to his wife from love for her son whom she does not love and whom she can never call by his name. And when Virginia is killed by a flying bomb, the child survives, Guy marries again and has two boys of his own. It is a vindication of his goodness, the goodness that he has discovered in himself late in the day.

But this is not the complete picture, and we must consider an issue that is peculiar to *Unconditional Surrender* alone, that of personal responsibility within the context of collective guilt. Whereas Julia, in her monologue by the fountain, expresses her guilt for her 'living in sin', Guy, in his period of service in Yugoslavia, realises his involvement in a collective failure to help the suffering Jews to whom he had promised help and who had been moved away following the objections of the partisans who considered the Jews to be receiving special treatment. This very much reflects the frustrations that Waugh felt during his time in Yugoslavia, frustrations that he now expresses many years later through Guy. Not only is Waugh aware that he is liable to be unpleasant to others and in his personal relationships, expressed in *The Ordeal of Gilbert Pinfold* in his question to himself: 'Why does everyone except me find it so easy to be nice?'.[76] He knows of his deeper problem which he expresses through the lips of Guy. Mme Kanyi, the Jewish woman whom he has been trying to help and with whose plight he sympathises, asks her rhetorical question: 'Is there any place that is free from evil?' She demonstrates that all countries have been involved in wanting war and says, confirming Waugh's conviction that war, far from revealing man's love of honour, brings out the dishonourable side of human nature:

> It seems to me that there was a will to war, a death
> wish, everywhere. Even good men thought their
> private honour could be satisfied by war. They could
> assert their manhood by killing and being killed. They

would accept hardships in recompense for having
been selfish and lazy [...] I knew Italians [...] who felt
this. Were there none in England?' In response Guy
confesses: 'God forgive me [...] I was one of them.[77]

Guy's renewed sense of commitment to serving God has intensified in him his awareness of personal involvement in the world's guilt. Stannard speaks of 'Crouchback's slow discovery of terrestrial impotence and spiritual vocation, his relationship to God, not man', and continues:

> Without charity and compassion, there could be no
> sanctity; the achievement of sanctity was the ultimate
> goal of devotion. But charity and compassion could be
> artfully constructed to defend failures of responsibility.
> Crouchback's ultimate wisdom involves his acceptance
> of guilt, of cowardly complicity in the face of evil.[78]

While we may feel that this is rather hard on Guy whose intentions and sympathies are always obvious, both he, and Waugh, are aware of the ultimate dilemma of the Christian, an acute awareness of our failings and our share in the world's guilt offset by our awareness of the power of Grace.

It remains for us now to return to Julia and Charles, and to consider the outcome as it affects the latter, who, after all, is the narrator and protagonist in Waugh's first great Catholic novel. Ironically, Julia has failed to see the change that the deathbed scene and 'conversion' of her father have wrought in Charles, a change that might have rendered her sacrifice unnecessary and might have meant that they could indeed have progressed together. She fails to grasp how Charles has understood her decision. 'Why should I be allowed to understand that, and not you, Charles?'.[79] And in his final recollections following his return to Brideshead, Charles prays 'an ancient, newly-learned form of words'.[80] It is as if he has come to a faith in an ancient tradition, but in what is for him a new formulation. He has said his prayer in the chapel, the chapel that had earlier been closed, but

234

where the lamp is burning once more. For Charles it now marks a new and unexpected beginning:

> Something quite remote from anything the builders intended has come out of their work, and out of the fierce little human tragedy in which I played; something none of us thought about at the time; a small red flame [...] the flame which the old knights saw from their tombs, which they saw put out; that flame burns again for other soldiers, far from home, farther [...] than Acre or Jerusalem. It could not have been lit but for the builders and the tragedians, and there I found it this morning, burning anew among the old stones.[81]

It has been said that 'out of all the tragedy, and justifying it, one good is seen emerging – the conversion of the narrator'.[82] The family has been scattered and has even dissolved physically. However, if we recall Cordelia's last conversation with Charles, in which she spoke of the closing of the chapel, she quotes the words from the first verse of Lamentations: *Quomodo sedet sola civitas* ('How deserted lies the city'), a lamentation on the 'process of disintegration metaphorically represented by the disbanding of the Flytes [...] the departure from Brideshead in all its voluptuous beauty'.[83] But in the chapel that day of his return, Charles recalls the words from Lamentations in a nostalgic look at the decayed tradition. 'And yet [...]', thinks Charles, 'that is not the last word.'[84] Ironically, the soul of the newcomer, Charles the 'poor agnostic' in Cordelia's words,[85] has arisen out of the ruins, joining the tradition of the Faith of previous generations and also the rest of the family now serving in Palestine (according to the old retainer, Nanny Hawkins[86]) and even reaching out beyond to the rest of the world. It has been a regeneration, even a resurrection from the disintegration of the past. There is here a pre-echo of what will be fulfilled in Helena, far away in the Holy Land where the Faith began and was manifest in the Cross. It is the unexpected event that the builders did not foresee is this quiet moment in the chapel so many years after Charles had last seen his beloved.

Conclusion

However, surely Charles had already found this new flame amidst the turmoil of that experience on that fateful day when his beloved gives him up for God and his return to Brideshead enables him to gain perspective and acceptance. But who knows how the Spirit of God moves in us frail human beings? Patey has pointed out justifiably how Charles' whole experience has been a progression in love. 'His loves form a series of steps [...] from Sebastian through Julia to God.'[87] At all events, his experience, and that of Sebastian, Julia and their father, confirm Cordelia's earlier prophetic words when she speaks of the 'unseen hook and [...] invisible line which is long enough to let him wander to the ends of the earth and still to bring him back with a twitch upon the thread'.[88]

Yet, finally, a distinction should be made between the work of the divine Spirit in the hearts of Julia, Sebastian and her father who had lapsed from the family tradition that Lady Marchmain and Lord Brideshead had upheld, but have now returned, like the fish caught on the 'unseen hook and [...] invisible line' hauled in to land by the 'twitch on the thread' and the new work of the Holy Spirit in the hearts of Charles, Helena and indeed of Waugh himself, who have no tradition of Faith to hold to before faith claims them too. And still there is Guy who never lapses, but remains in the Faith with a heart heavy with defeat, observing the formalities, until his moment of commitment and fulfilment comes. It certainly appears that, no matter what our spiritual position may be, whether we are ardent or lukewarm, new or old in the faith, God is present to welcome us home.

This article was first published in *The Heythrop Journal,* November 2011.

Endnotes

1   Evelyn Waugh, *Brideshead Revisited* (Penguin, 1962).

2   *The Observer*, 27 May 2007.

3   Interview with David Lister, *The Independent,* December 2002.

4   Evelyn Waugh, *The Ordeal of Gilbert Pinfold* (Penguin, 1998), 5.

5   Waugh, *Brideshead,* 36.

6   Waugh, *Brideshead,* 87.

7   Waugh, *Brideshead,* 192.

8   Waugh, *Brideshead,* 158.

9   Waugh, *Brideshead,* 140.

10 Waugh, *Brideshead,* 314.

11 Donat Gallagher (ed.), *The Essays, Articles and Reviews of Evelyn Waugh* (London: Methuen, 1983), 103-4.

12 Radio interview with Stephen Black (series *Personal Call,* BBC Overseas series, September 1953).

13 Waugh, *Pinfold,* 8.

14 Mark Amory (ed.), *Letters of Evelyn Waugh* (Phoenix, 1995), 185.

15 Waugh, *Brideshead,* 185.

16 G.K. Chesterton, *Father Brown* (Wordsworth Classics, 1992), 48.

17 Waugh, *Brideshead,* 212.

18 Waugh, *Brideshead,* 293.

19 Waugh, *Brideshead,* 207.

20 Waugh, *Brideshead,* 213.

21 Waugh, *Brideshead,* 247.

22 Waugh, *Brideshead*, 272.

23 Waugh, *Brideshead*, 273.

24 Waugh, *Brideshead*, 274.

25 Waugh, *Brideshead*, 276.

26 Waugh, *Brideshead*, 296.

27 Waugh, *Brideshead*, 324.

28 Evelyn Waugh, *Helena* (London: Penguin, 1963).

29 Amory (ed.), *Letters*, 206.

30 Amory (ed.), *Letters*, 339.

31 Waugh, *Helena*, 16.

32 Waugh, *Helena*, 39-40.

33 Waugh, *Helena*, 83.

34 Waugh, *Helena*, 84.

35 Martin Stannard, *Evelyn Waugh: No Abiding Place* (London: Dent, 1992), 279.

36 Waugh, *Helena*, 88.

37 Waugh, *Helena*, 89.

38 Waugh, *Helena*, 122.

39 Waugh, *Helena*, 89.

40 Waugh, *Helena*, 89.

41 Waugh, *Helena*, 90.

42 Amory (ed.), *Letters*, 339.

43 Waugh, *Helena*, 127.

44 Waugh, *Helena*, 128.

45 Amory (ed.), *Letters*, 341.

46 Waugh, *Helena*, 144.

47 Waugh, *Helena*, 156.

48 Waugh, *Helena*, 125.

49 Stannard, *Evelyn Waugh*, 278.

50 Waugh, *Brideshead*, 272-8.

51 Waugh, *Helena*, 159.

52 Evelyn Waugh, *Men at Arms, Officers and Gentlemen*, and *Unconditional Surrender*, published in one volume as *The*

Sword of Honour Trilogy (Penguin 1984). All references to these novels are to this volume.

53 Amory (ed.), *Letters,* 141.

54 Amory (ed.), *Letters,* 463.

55 Amory (ed.), *Letters,* 215.

56 Selina Hastings, *Evelyn Waugh – A Biography* (London: Sinclair-Stevenson, 1954), 547.

57 Douglas Lane Patey, *The Life of Evelyn Waugh* (Blackwell, 1988), 212.

58 Waugh, *Men at Arms,* 28.

59 Waugh, *Men at Arms,* 16.

60 Waugh, *Men at Arms,* 13.

61 Waugh, *Men at Arms,* 20.

62 Waugh, *Men at Arms,* 132.

63 Amory (ed.), *Letters,* 188.

64 Amory (ed.), *Letters,* 192.

65 Amory (ed.), *Letters,* 363-4.

66 Evelyn Waugh, *Unconditional Surrender,* 398.

67 Waugh, *Surrender,* 400.

68 Waugh, *Surrender,* 438.

69 Waugh, *Surrender,* 438 and Michael Davie (ed.), *The Diaries of Evelyn Waugh* (Weidenfeld and Nicholson, 1976), 722.

70 Waugh, *Surrender,* 438.

71 Waugh, *Surrender,* 400.

72 Thomas Keneally, *Schindler's Ark* (Sceptre, 1986), 52.

73 Amory (ed.), *Letters,* 339.

74 Waugh, *Helena,* 144.

75 Waugh, *Helena,* 145.

76 Waugh, *Pinfold,* 23.

77 Waugh, *Surrender,* 565-6.

78 Stannard, *Evelyn Waugh,* 442.

79 Waugh, *Brideshead,* 324.

80 Waugh, *Brideshead,* 330.

81 Waugh, *Brideshead,* 331.

82 D. O'Donnell, *Maria Cross: Imaginative Patterns in a Group of Modern Catholic Writers* (Chatto & Windus, 1954), 127.

83 Waugh, *Brideshead,* 212 and Hastings, *Evelyn Waugh,* 400.

84 Waugh, *Brideshead,* 331.

85 Waugh, *Brideshead,* 212.

86 Waugh, *Brideshead,* 329.

87 Patey, *Life of Waugh,* 236.

88 Waugh, *Brideshead,* 212.